THE BOSS LIFE

Are you living a purpose-driven life that you designed, or are you living by default? Are you waiting for the "perfect time" to make your dream a reality, but the right time never seems to come?

It's time to fire your fear, build your faith, and become the BOSS of your own life! Through The Boss Life Podcast *and the online course* The Boss Life Blueprint, *Stefanie Peters will be bringing you exclusive interviews from powerhouse entrepreneurs, social influencers, and inspirational guests on how you can up-level your leadership, create multiple streams of income, and unapologetically own your success.*

Get yourself on the FAST track today and check it out at www.TheBossLife.tv

You only live once; you might as well be a boss.

THE BOSS LIFE
Blueprint

Stefanie Peters

The Boss Life Blueprint © copyright 2020 by Stefanie Peters. All rights reserved. No part of this book may be reproduced in any form whatsoever, by photography or xerography or any other means, by broadcast or transmission, by translation into any kind of language, nor by recording electronically or otherwise, without permission in writing from the author, except by a reviewer, who may quote brief passages in critical articles or reviews.

ISBN: 978-0-578-53056-7

23 22 21 20 19   5 4 3 2 1

Cover design by Crystal Stautzenberger
Interior design by Ann Aubitz, FuzionPress.com

Published by Boss Life Media

Boss Life Media

To order visit www.thebosslife.tv
Reseller discounts also available.

INTRODUCING

THE BOSS LIFE BLUEPRINT

Three months from TODAY, your life could be completely transformed—or, you could find yourself exactly where you are now. It's a choice! You have the power to be in a completely different place mentally, physically, spiritually, and financially, but you have to take ACTION on your dreams. Are you ready to rock the next twelve weeks? Let's do this!

Each week we'll go through four steps:

1. We'll read a powerful Boss Bold Breakthrough story.
2. We'll discover the Boss Bold Power Principle that created the breakthrough.
3. I'll lead you through creating your own Boss Bold Power Move based on what was learned, backed with affirmations and prayer.
4. I'll help you create your Boss Bold Power Habit to break you through to the next level!

CONTENTS

THE BOSS EXPERIENCE
Your Twelve-Week Plan

Week 1	Envision Your Ultimate Boss Life	11
Week 2	Dominate Your Doubts	37
Week 3	Dare to Jump	55
Week 4	Become a Goal Digger	67
Week 5	Chisel the Goal in Granite	87
Week 6	Ignite Fearless Focus	97
Week 7	Fail Fast and Furious	113
Week 8	Master Your Mindset	129
Week 9	Build Your Dream Tribe	147
Week 10	Become a Legend and Leave Your Legacy	171
Week 11	My Top 100 Live List	191
Week 12	The Boss Life Blueprint	204

LETTER

TO MY FELLOW BOSSES:

Hello Boss,

I am so blessed that you decided to join me on this adventure of a lifetime, and I applaud you for taking a powerful first step toward shifting into a growth mindset. It's exciting to team up with you on this journey, taking your life to a whole new level! It'll be a blast, but just know there will be growing pains along the way. Nerves and doubt are normal, but as long as you breathe through it and dedicate all of this to the Man Upstairs, nothing can stop you.

When I was brainstorming with my team on how best to equip you to design your ultimate Boss Life plan of action, we all agreed we didn't want just another "inspirational" book you read once, get excited about in the moment, and then place on the shelf to be forgotten. So, instead, we decided to create a goal-setter's guide that will serve as a quick reference for when you feel stuck or exhausted and need reminders and re-inspiration. This is not a one-and-done read-through inspirational journal.

In my previous book, *Unleash Your Lady Boss*, I shared ten keys to unlocking your ultimate Boss Life and igniting the greatness within. Now, with this "Boss Life Blueprint" workbook, we are taking it a step further and equipping you to execute each Boss Bold move and take MASSIVE action toward your dreams. Again, this is a *work*book, so get ready, roll up your sleeves, and put on your Boss boots!

Stefanie Peters

> *"If you're going to answer the call and you're going to transform and you're going to change, get ready. It is not a day at the beach."*
> —Elizabeth Gilbert

Here's to firing your fear, building your faith, and becoming the Boss of your own life!

Your Cheerleader of God-Sized Dreams,

Stefanie Peters

P.S. Be sure to go to www.TheBossLife.tv to download the PDF version of the blueprint and strategy which will equip you to get the most out of this book!

CHAPTER 1

ENVISION YOUR ULTIMATE BOSS LIFE

*"Vision is the most powerful weapon
in the leader's arsenal."*

–Bill Hybels

Week 1

BOSS BREAKTHROUGH

"Ten thousand people are cheering for me. I am being interviewed by the CEO of a billion-dollar company. Holy wow! I'm a 22-year-old blonde gal who just shattered the glass ceiling. I'm pretty sure more adrenaline has shot through my body in the last ten minutes than in the last ten months. I'm humbled and jazzed beyond belief to have led my team to break the sales record of all time. The Inc. 500 company awards me an honor few will ever receive. I literally pinch myself. Though I'm extremely nervous, I decide to embrace the moment and power through. Under the hot stage lights, television cameras, and in front of thousands of trailblazers, my CEO declares with pride and amazement:

'Stefanie, you're the youngest female executive director in the 25-year history of the company. You've created enough residual income that, by retirement age, you'll have earned 6.4 million dollars. I know what a hard worker you are, and you're growing like crazy, so I know you won't stop here. You will actually earn millions more. Congratulations. You've paved the way for countless people, inspired the masses, and led from the heart. 'You're my hero!'"

"That moment changed my life forever. I knew it was my time. But I didn't know I was destined to lead a movement. So if you want to change your life and become a commander on a mission, you're reading the right book. If you feel there has to be more to life, take heart. If you're committed to being the boss of your future, kick those fears to the curb and let's get after it!"

You're on the brink of your breakthrough!

Since the release of my best-selling book, *Unleash Your Lady Boss*, I've stayed quite the busy gal, and much has happened. I created multiple new streams of residual income revolving around my passion zones, hosted "Boss Life Breakthrough Events" throughout the U.S., and produced an online course to empower YOU to write YOUR own story.

Sounds like a charmed life, right? But let's get REAL for a moment: there's an entire behind-the-scenes portion of the journey that few have seen. For example, a person attending one of my recent events could have seen a packed-house success with legendary sponsors like Calvin Klein and Fabletics, but wouldn't know about the unceremonious rejection I got slammed with from another. Yep, I got rejected by a sponsor in a pretty comical way that was not so funny at the time—but more on that later.

In today's social media society, we're bombarded with images of people's highlight reels but very rarely see the time spent on the practice field. So many people fall into the trap of comparing themselves to an image of their peers that doesn't tell the whole story. Recently a friend of mine, who had just been posting that day about how fabulously her business was going, called me devastated and in tears. Even though by all appearances she was "keeping up with the Kardashians," the reality was that she felt woefully unfulfilled—a victim and participant in the social media illusion.

"Never underestimate the power of dreams and the influence of the human spirit. We are all the same in this notion: The potential for greatness lives within each of us."
—Wilma Rudolph

I want to expose this and other myths we believe about success, uncover the truth of what it takes to make your dreams a reality, and, most importantly, empower you to get out of your own head and take ACTION on the dream placed on your heart. Together, we are going to layout your Boss Life Blueprint so you are crystal clear on your purpose, know how to execute on your God-sized dreams, and are able to outwit the challenges along the way.

> The purpose of this personal power plan is to bring you behind the scenes to what it takes to ignite your dreams and build the life you desire.

I want to expose the illusions and deceptions that paralyze and keep you from attaining your goals. Ultimately, I want to set you up for success, significance, and living a life you have dreamed of but couldn't quite figure out how to access.

I have hosted many empowerment seminars since the release of my first book, and the feedback has been phenomenal. I've been so grateful for how the book has transformed others' lives and, in turn, affected mine. It's been a wonderful journey. However, not long after the book was published, I received a tap on the shoulder from the Big Guy upstairs, and He downloaded yet another vision into my heart. "Oh boy, here we go again," I thought with a sense of excitement. Right when you accomplish a God-sized dream,

He will drop another, expand your vision, and keep tapping on the door of your heart until you answer the call.

When I was having my quiet time that morning, I heard a still, small voice say, "I want you to reach the masses with my message of hope. It's time to go Boss BOLD on sharing your faith and how this gives you the strength and confidence to rock it out in your business. I want you to share powerhouse stories from high-level influencers on how they achieved their success, extract the powerful principles, and equip people to take massive ACTION on their God-sized dreams."

So, here we are!

I have been told many times by multiple publishers not to touch the topic of religion when it comes to my writing. Well, let's get something straight: I'm not here to promote religion. I am, however, all about my relationship with God and giving Him the credit for the strength He has given me to soar to new heights in my life and business.

> **Let my language be bold and clear right now as I tell you that you didn't run across this personal power plan by accident.**

I don't believe in coincidence, chance, or happenstance. I do believe in providence, I do believe in divine intervention, and I do believe you are reading this for a bigger reason than you may realize. Here's what I know: God brings people together for such a time as this. I am always praying for supernatural and divine connections and downloads from all directions.

So, congratulations!

YOU ARE PART OF THE BIGGER PLAN, AND THIS MAY BE THE ANSWER FOR WHICH YOU'VE BEEN PRAYING.

I constantly pray that God will put my books in the right hands at the right time, because when you put the right book in the right hands at the right time, miracles happen.

> The right book can pull someone out of depression, plant a seed, solve a problem, meet a need, transform a life, change a heart, ignite a God-sized dream, or, dare I say, rally a revival.

This is why I do what I do. This is why I am up at 4:50 on a storming Tuesday morning, typing away at my computer. It's because I know this could be your tipping point; this could be your answer; this could be the miracle you have been praying for.

Trust that your Father in heaven knows and loves you fully, beyond what you can even comprehend, beyond human capacity. Trust that no matter your past or current circumstances, He has a phenomenal plan for your life. Trust that He can use the unique successes and challenges He's led me through to help you along the way. I believe I was put on this planet to be your cheerleader of God-sized dreams, and I KNOW you have what it takes to make your dreams a reality. So, are you ready to begin a new era in your life? Then, let's do this!

"Success is never owned, it is only rented; and rent is due every day."

YOUR BOSS LIFE

First off, before we start thinking big picture,
we need to define what being a "Boss" means.

Here is my definition of a Boss:

Bosses are leaders who shine their light to the world through actively pursuing their God-given potential. They know when to throw punches and when to roll with them. They never allow others to determine their destiny or detour their direction. They feel the fear, confront it, and grab the pen to write their own story. They pursue their purpose to inspire and empower others to unleash their greatness within.

There are many ways you can be a Boss. It's important to define the type of Boss you want to become so you know what your target is.

- Maybe it's to be the best mother or father you can be.
- Maybe it's to become the CEO at the company where you work.
- Maybe it's to make an impact for a non-profit organization.
- Maybe it's to own your very own company.
- Maybe it's to invent a new product that will change lives.
- Maybe it's to fulfill a lifelong dream of becoming a doctor.
- Maybe it's to be a light for other people to know God.
- Maybe it's to finally learn to love and appreciate yourself.
- Maybe it's...YOU fill in the blank! It's your life; own it!

It doesn't have to be earth-shattering, but it has to light you up and ignite your soul.

YOUR BOSS LIFE

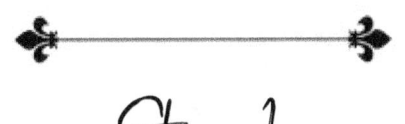

Don't turn this page until you write something down. It doesn't have to be perfect or even complete. You can always add more to it later, but write something now!

1. Create your definition of a Boss:

   _____
   _____
   _____
   _____
   _____
   _____

2. Decide today that you will become the Boss of your own life! What will being your own Boss allow you the freedom to do? Take a moment to dream in the space below and then turn the page to sign your very own Boss Bold contract!

   _____
   _____
   _____
   _____
   _____
   _____

BOSS BOLD CONTRACT

"A real decision is measured by the fact that you've taken new action. If there's no action, you haven't truly decided."
—Tony Robbins

It all starts with a decision!
I hereby declare that today I have become the Boss of my own life!
I am not waiting until someone tells me I am ready or worthy.
I am giving myself permission to grab the pen and write my own story!
Today I am making a commitment to work like everything depends on me and pray like everything depends on God because I know it does.

I will commit to work hard, take action, and be accountable to myself and my power partner (accountability teammate). I won't be too hard on myself, but I won't let myself off the hook.

I understand that when I follow the Boss Bold principles, I will be successful and significant in the lives I impact. I will achieve my ultimate Boss Life and ignite the greatness that is within me now.

With Stefanie's signature below, I know that she will do everything she can to make sure I'm successful, so I promise to step into my genius zone and unapologetically own my greatness.

Name: _____ date: _____

Stefanie Peters

CONSIDER THIS...

Envision your Boss Life Blueprint in your mind's eye.

You can't build a house without blueprints or a plan. Well, I guess you could—but you probably wouldn't want to live in a house tossed together without intention. The same goes for your life; you can live life without a vision, but my guess is that you will end up frustrated, flat-lined, and feeling purposeless as you bump along.

I want to share an excerpt from my previous book because it emphasizes so well the need for vision.

"I believe we've all been given fabulous, life-changing ideas and a unique song of our own. But we have to believe it. And we have to envision it. Without a vision, our soul withers, we dim our light, and we become cynical.

The Bible says that where there's no vision, the people perish (Proverbs 29:18). Research shows that the longer the members of an ancestry group have been in the U.S., the less likely they are to become millionaires, because they acclimate to a high-consumption lifestyle. On the other hand, first-generation Americans tend to be self-employed, and that increases their chance of becoming millionaires by seven times. What makes foreign-born U.S. residents seven times more likely to achieve their dreams? They see the opportunity and seize the day! I believe it's too easy for Americans to become complacent. We forget the incredible opportunity we have to dream larger-than-life victories for ourselves. Your life is a stunning masterpiece you can paint with your own brush. But you can't paint without a dream."

Unleash Your Lady Boss, p. 19, 20

Can you believe that? We can literally shift the trajectory of our lives by making the choice to run towards opportunity.

I love the way my mentor, Jim Rohn, says it:

"If you don't design your own life plan, chances are you will fall into someone else's life plan. And guess what they have planned for you? Not much."
—Jim Rohn

If that doesn't light a fire inside your soul to get serious about your vision, then I don't know what will. However, since you are reading this book, I have a strong feeling you are ready to live fully and fight for those dreams that have pressed on your heart for years upon years.

You've probably heard the quote from Andrew Murphy:

"You are confined only by the walls you build yourself."
—Andrew Murphy

Oftentimes, the walls we build around ourselves end up as a fortress of self-doubt and disbelief. However, what if I told you that you can tear down your walls and create an open space of limitless potential? When you see your dream vividly in your mind, you can create a blueprint and activate your faith to make it a reality!

God wants you to see a bigger, bolder picture of your life than what you are experiencing today. A baby step in a forward direction will add up to leaps and bounds over time. Not taking any intentional action will keep you right where you are, so move! This is your story, and the next chapter can be a repeat of the last or the start of a best-seller. I dare you to become the hero you have been waiting for.

BOSS LIFE HACK

"If you've always wanted to travel or go on an exotic trip to Bali, pack your suitcase, create the itinerary, and start planning how to make it happen. If you've always wanted to start your own business, it's time to buy the domain name for your website. If you want to write a book, it's time to see that book in your hands, published, and making its impact. Write your first chapter or even the first paragraph!"

"If you want to launch a blog, imagine that blog live and in color doing its thing and being shared by millions of engaged followers! Write your first post by the end of this week. Don't wait. The word dream is a verb; dreams are not meant to be stagnant ideas in your brilliant brain."
(Unleash Your Lady Boss, p. 17).

KICK OUT YOUR BAGGAGE

It is time!

Whose voices do you hear saying you're not good enough?
What stories are you telling yourself of who you "should" be?
#stopshouldingonyourself

_____
_____
_____

What messages were given to you when you were young that told you who you are? Are you still trying to live up to your parents' standards? What expectations have others put on you? Is this serving you?

_____
_____
_____

Can you remember when someone or some experience first handed you the baggage you've been carrying around?

_____
_____
_____

BOSS BOLD POWER MOVE

This is your time to dream!

It's not up to someone else to tell you who you are or what you're capable of—that's your job.

Take a moment to close your eyes, think about your life, and evaluate from where you've come. Now, thank God for the lessons, bless and release the past, and kick out the baggage holding you back from your greatness. Decide that today is the day that everything changes.

What story is stopping you from moving to the next level?
_____
_____
_____

Where are you leaking energy?
_____
_____
_____

What healthy boundaries do you need to enforce?
_____
_____
_____

LET'S GET REAL

It's okay if you don't have a crystal-clear vision for your life yet, but start writing anyway. Take five minutes every morning to record your visions in a journal. Do not get caught up in feeling like you have to have the perfect plan or words. Write without an agenda.

I know how it is when your project (e.g., book, course, business idea) is etched so deeply into your soul. You want so badly to put it out to the world, but you've been waiting for the perfect timing, situation, client, etc., to come along. Don't fall into this trap! Preparation, yes, but perfection, no. Figure it out along the way, get uncomfortable and messy, be confident in the fact that what you need is already inside of you.

> "In the journal I do not just express myself more openly than I could to any person; I create myself."
> —Susan Sontag

Okay, so go ahead and commit to a time of the day that you will allow yourself to journal without an agenda, a time that you will dream and dare yourself to breathe life into your God-given desires through written expression.

Time each day that I will journal: _____

BOSS BOLD PRINCIPLE

This is the first thing I ask when creating something or working on a project/business/career:

"Who needs this, and how will it make their life and/or business easier?"

I want you to release any expectations of what you think should be written and simply allow your thoughts and imagination to flow effortlessly from your pen to the paper. Journaling does not have to be intimidating or boring—it can be a safe place and empowering. Journaling has unlocked God-sized visions for me, and I know it will do the same for you. Today is the day that you can put this powerful habit into practice. Pick up that pen, Boss!

There have been times in my life when my vision is crystal clear. Yet, there are other times when "life" has happened, and I don't know which end is up. Regardless of what season you are in, always look up, take heart, and hold fast to God's promises.

In Jeremiah 29:11 it declares: "For I know the plans I have for you; plans to prosper you and not to harm you, plans to give you hope and a future."

The vision comes first;
the ideas come second!
Write it all down!

What did you dream about pursuing as a young child?
___
___
___

What excites you now?
___
___
___

What do you do that causes you to forget to eat?
___
___
___

What keeps you awake at night?
___
___
___

ENVISION YOUR ULTIMATE BOSS LIFE

Dial it in!

One-Year Vision

Imagine it's December 31 of next year, and you are at a New Year's Eve party. It has been the best year of your life yet! You are reflecting on all the phenomenal things that have happened, goals you have achieved, and lives you have impacted! Write here in detail what has occurred over the past year.

_____
_____
_____
_____
_____
_____
_____
_____
_____
_____
_____
_____

ENVISION YOUR ULTIMATE BOSS LIFE

Game on, Boss!

Five-Year Vision

Now, let's continue envisioning the life ahead, but let's expand it to five years from now. Where do you live? Who are you living with? How do you feel? How are you making your impact? Did you write that book, launch that podcast, or start that blog? Did you start that business or go on your dream vacation? Did you raise money for the cause that has been tugging at your heart? What type of income are you making? What is God calling you to do?

Again, this is your time to let your imagination run wild! Don't hold back! We will rein it in later, create specific timelines, and shift from dreams to goals and deadlines. But for now, just DREAM!

_____
_____
_____
_____
_____
_____
_____
_____

ENVISION YOUR ULTIMATE BOSS LIFE

My favorite part!

Ten-Year Vision

For this exercise, find a quiet place, clear your mind, and relax. Come with me and imagine, if money had nothing to do with your life, what would you do with your time? Are you in a passionate marriage, raising incredible children? What does your relationship with God look like?

Are you building a legacy? If so, what are you leaving for your children and the next generation? If your children watched your actions, would it inspire them to pursue their passions? What do you want to be remembered for in life? Remember, it is your God-given gift and responsibility to do just that!

Don't judge anything that comes up. This is a no-limits zone, so dream big, Boss! We will get more specifics later, but for now just let your imagination run wild. Describe what you see, hear, and feel in your ideal Boss Life.

_____

_____

_____

_____

_____

_____

BOSS BOLD POWER HABIT
Stefanie Peter's Power Habit:

Every morning during prayer time, I thank God for His blessings and declare my dreams out loud. I then visualize myself having already achieved them. Your mind must arrive at your destination before your life does.

It's your turn! Take a few minutes to create your morning Power Habit routine below.

Example: Committing to writing five things that you are grateful for every day for the next 30 days.

_____
_____
_____
_____
_____
_____
_____
_____
_____
_____
_____
_____

AFFIRMATIONS

I declare that today is my day to glorify God and pursue the purpose He has placed on my heart. I am putting massive action behind my faith and taking Boss Bold steps toward my destiny!

I am not only capable of pursuing my God-sized dreams, but I am equipped because my Creator has called me. I believe that past circumstances do not define my future reality. I am ready to step towards my future, and I am prepared and confident.

I am worthy of opportunity. I am more than enough. My life will change lives.

PRAYER

Dear God,
today I ask that you impact the way in which I see my future. Place dreams in my heart that are beyond my wildest imagination—dreams that will serve others and glorify You in the highest. I ask for a posture of humility and confidence. Lord, use me as a vessel and give me eyes to see what You see and ears to hear Your voice clearly. Guide my hand and heart in all that I do. Help me not to shrink back, but to shine brightly so that others will see You and see more possibility for their lives. I pray for Your favor and protection. I pray You would grow and stretch me throughout this journey, and remind me of my worth and capabilities.
Amen.

RESOURCES

1. *Soar! Build Your Vision from the Ground Up* by TD Jakes

2. *Visioneering: God's Blueprint for Developing and Maintaining Personal Vision* by Andy Stanley

3. *Hello, Tomorrow! The Transformational Power of Vision* by Cindy Trimm

> Don't take the plan everyone says you're supposed to follow. Instead, choose the greater purpose destined for you.
>
> #GoBossBold
> @LadyBoss_SP

CHAPTER 2

DOMINATE YOUR DOUBTS

"The chances you take, the people you meet, the people you love, the faith that you have—that's what's going to define you."

−Denzel Washington

Week 2

Nicole's Story

Nicole was abandoned by her biological father before she was even born, but that was just the beginning of her difficulties. At age ten she was molested by a neighbor, and when the news leaked out, she became a social outcast at her school. Yet, through the devastation she experienced, she had an encounter with Jesus Christ and dedicated her life to Him. That decision allowed her to overcome the upcoming trauma because her foundation was solid. A few years later, at age 13, she was raped. By age 17, she found herself an unwed, pregnant woman. As an adult she suffered severe physical abuse by her first husband, a man who had become drug-addicted and violent. Eventually, she was left a single mom with a young son, divorced, bankrupt, and working to survive.

If such a beginning wouldn't give reason to doubt oneself, I don't know what would. Nicole was devastated and didn't know where to turn.

However, she started going to church every Sunday morning and night, and she began connecting with God in a way she never had before. Once she began to seek God simply because she desired a relationship with Him, that's when God brought the right *him* along.

Nicole and David Crank were soon married, and together they began pastoring a church of 180 members. The congregation would eventually grow to over 18,000 members. In 2016, *Outreach Magazine* recognized Faith Church as the 58th largest church in America. It is now ranked as one of the top ten most influential churches in America by *Newsmax* magazine.

Genesis 50:20—"You intended to harm me, but God intended it for good to accomplish what is now being done, the saving of many lives."

Nicole's Story

Now, Pastor Nicole shares her story with countless others to help them through their trials. She has been featured weekly on ABC, CBS, and FOX TV in West Palm Beach, Florida, as well as ABC, CBS, NBC, and CW television networks in St. Louis, Missouri. Nicole has also appeared as a guest several times on international television networks like Daystar and TBN. Most recently, she was asked by the BVOVN network to host her own show and is currently hosting The Nicole Crank Show.

Yes, the enemy intended to destroy Nicole, but God had a greater plan to use her gifts and talents to minister to thousands of people all around the world. God has a plan for you as well.

But, does it sometimes seem like you aren't enough or that there is no plan for you? Have you ever felt alone, rejected, riddled with doubt, and denied? I surely have, many times. Being rejected was honestly one of my biggest fears for so many years! But when you understand Whose you are and focus on performing for an audience of One, it leaves no room for feeling like you aren't enough because HE is enough.

God bridges the gaps. He'll make a way when it looks like there is no way. Here's the deal: even when things have been going phenomenally, in an instant, DOUBT can pop up out of nowhere. It's your choice to let your doubts dominate, or to take control of your thoughts, tell them who's Boss, and dominate those damn doubts! I challenge you to choose the latter.

Doubts arise, and the enemy will use people, circumstances, and situations to try to undermine God's plan for your life. But the enemy can't stop the ultimate Boss Life God has ordained for you if you don't allow it. The enemy comes to kill, steal, and destroy, but Jesus came that we may have LIFE in abundance to the full until it OVERFLOWS! (John 10:10).

"You're wishin' too much, baby. You gotta stop wearing your wishbone where your backbone oughta be."
—Elizabeth Gilbert

It took Elizabeth Gilbert (author of *Eat Pray Love*, *Big Magic*, and other titles) seven years before her career as an author took off—seven years! During that time, she worked as a cook, a waitress, and many other day jobs to support what she referred to as her "real job," writing.

Do what you need to do to support yourself and your family, but don't quit your Boss Life. Dream, and don't let anyone else strip you of your destiny.

When you think of the simple phrase,

There is more.

What truths begin echoing in your heart? When in your life have you persevered beyond the odds? What "fight" in you is dying to come out so that you can push through and move further and faster towards your dream?

Take a few moments to reflect on the next page.

BOSS BOLD PRINCIPLE

As horrific as Pastor Nicole's early story was, it also gives us much hope. God was faithful in her situation, but she had to do her part to fight through to the other side.

So many people hear her story and are in awe of how she overcame the odds. Others may ask: How can I dominate the doubts in my situation? How do I get out of my own head? How can I create confidence when I'm scared to move forward?

First, I want you to know that I understand the feeling. I have faced times of looming doubt and still go through bouts from time to time. Just read my first book—Lord knows my doubts almost flatlined me. But now, whenever I feel doubt trying to creep in, I go Boss BOLD!

Dominate your doubts.

I have created a powerful formula to get you out of your head and into FAST action by going "BOLD!" "What's that," you ask? Let me explain! Turn that page, and let's get started!

"God placed the best things on the other side of terror; on the other side of fear are the best things in life."

—Will Smith

HERE'S HOW I DEAL WITH MY DOUBTS AND DOMINATE THEM!

Step 1

BURN the lies that are holding you back from your destiny, and toss away the ashes! Defy, deny, and discard all the negative, fearful, and doubtful thoughts in your mind. Stand strong against them. Do not listen to or give these lies even a moment's attention.

Step 2

OWN your power and speak the truth! Write down or print out encouraging words of truth, and post them where you can see and declare them every morning. Also, read and speak them out loud any time your mind is under attack. Take your power back, and own your greatness!

Step 3

LEAD with heart! Social media can be an incredible tool, but it can also mess a Boss up if we don't focus on the right thing. If we start to compare and feel unqualified, inferior, or anxious and fearful, we are stripped of our power. We must constantly center ourselves, and GRATITUDE is one of the best ways to do just that!

What you focus on expands, so it's crucial to concentrate on possibilities, impact, purpose, and the wonderful things that are happening in your life right now. You can't be fearful, anxious, and grateful at the same time. It's easy to fall into the trap of negativity or comparing yourself with others on social media, so it's important always to be mindful and thankful for all the blessings we have in our lives.

Step 4

DOMINATE your doubts with power declarations, affirmations, and scriptures!
FEELING READY?

BOSS BOLD POWER MOVE
Burn the lies.

I believe your past does not define your future, and you can be and do whatever you want when your intentions are pure. I know you can choose to become a dreamer any second of the day and, just as quickly, become a doer of your dreams. It's possible for you to give up on limits and give in to the idea of possibility.

So, let's get granular, detailed, and specific. List the lies that are swirling around in your head that aren't serving you and are holding you back from your greatness. What lies are renting space in your head?

Here are some examples of typical lies I have heard:
- I am not smart enough to start that business.
- I need to lose ten pounds before I start shooting videos for my business.
- I can't go all-in for my goal; my friends will think I am nuts and leave me.
- My dad says it'll never work. What am I doing?

As I said before, whatever you focus on expands, and a boss focuses on truth instead of lies. You need to know, deep in your heart, that your steps on this earth are being crafted by a Creator who has massive plans for you. But even so, that does not mean that the enemy is going to stop trying to deter your divine direction. It is up to you to call him out and declare,

"Not today, Satan!"

BOSS BOLD POWER MOVE

It is easiest to recognize the lies in your life when you are aware of them. So, I want you to take the next five minutes to write down every "lie" that you've ever believed to be true about yourself. It may be something someone said 15 years ago or something you spoke over yourself 15 minutes ago. Next, replace that lie with a truth.

Example:
Lie: I am lazy.
Truth: I am motivated to excel in the things that I am most passionate about.

LIES	TRUTHS

BOSS BOLD POWER MOVE

Now that you've written down all those lies, it's time to cross over and list the TRUTH. It's time to transition from the fixed mindset to the faith mindset, Boss! Your mind will try to play tricks on you constantly, and the best way to fight back against lies is with the truth. Take command of your mind when those negative thoughts pop up, and speak the truth—out loud!

Own your power and speak the truth.

Confront those lies with truths! Remember the lies I listed previously that I've heard? Well, here's the actual truth for each one:

- I am smart! Everything is "figure-out-able." God (and maybe a little help from Google) can always get me to where I need to be.
- I am enough just the way I am. I will continue to work on my wellness but will not put my life on hold or wait for the perfect time to propel my life and business forward.
- I will not downgrade my dreams to fit in with my friends.
- I am upgrading my goals to match my destiny, and my real friends support this. Divine connections and friendships appear when I act on my vision.
- I respect and honor my parents' opinions, but I know that, ultimately, opinions don't pay my bills.
- I cannot run my life according to what other people think. I've done my homework and am willing to take a chance on me.

POWERHOUSE WORDS

Here are a couple favorite affirmations and advice
from my fellow author, Terri Savelle Foy:

"I will fight fear with a plan! My plan will override fear.
All out massive action cures all fear!"

"My spirit attracts God-inspired ideas that bring millions of souls
and millions of dollars into the kingdom of God."

You've got to reroute your focus. If your desire is to be debt-free, stop looking through every catalog with the newest fashion trends. Instead, focus on how wonderful it would feel to be debt free, and think of the options and freedom it would give you and your family. Start reading books like *The Total Money Makeover* by Dave Ramsey and get inspired by the life-changing stories of how financial freedom can affect the trajectory of your destiny.

Pro Tip—stop focusing on what you shouldn't be eating. Instead, start focusing on an image of your body at its best. You'll get results!

For extra credit,

Google a scripture to back up your truth!

LEAD WITH HEART

The depth of your praise determines the magnitude of your miracle!

List the top five things you are grateful for:

1. _____

2. _____

3. _____

4. _____

5. _____

Dominate your doubts with power declarations, affirmations, and scriptures!

Act as "if."

I'm not a big fan of the phrase, "Fake it till you make it," but I love the phrase, "*Faith* it till you *feel* it." Actually, I don't know if it's an established phrase—I may or may not have made it up—but it works great, so let's go with it!

Take a moment to reflect on your dreams and visualize them in vivid detail. Now, act as if your dreams have already happened, and live accordingly.

Life can knock the wind right out of you, so it's important to have powerful words of faith to battle back and power forward. Here are some examples of power declarations, affirmations, and scriptures you can use. You can also Google more or write out your own. Use your ten-, five- and one-year visualizations from Chapter 1 for inspiration.

DECLARATIONS AND AFFIRMATIONS

- I declare that God's plan for my life is coming to pass.
- I declare that I choose faith over fear.
- I declare that I have influence, I walk in authority, and I lead like a Boss.
- I am fully equipped to accomplish all that God has in store for me.
- I am a powerful business owner who walks in favor with God and man.

SCRIPTURE

Isaiah 40:31—"But those who trust in the LORD will find new strength. They will soar high on wings like eagles. They will run and not grow weary. They will walk and not faint."

"I AM" STATEMENTS

"I am" statements work. Below are five such statements that I wrote long ago which have since come true. They came true because I repeated them for years!

1. I am a best-selling author whose books change the trajectory of people's lives.

2. I am the host of The Boss Life Podcast, which inspires the masses to take action on their God-sized dreams.

3. I am a high-level business coach who attracts and leads purpose-driven leaders.

4. I am a successful real estate investor.

5. I am an national speaker who helps transform people's lives with a powerful faith-based message.

BOSS BOLD POWER HABIT

Create five "I am" statements, and declare them out loud daily!

List your five "I am" statements here:

1. _____

2. _____

3. _____

4. _____

5. _____

Going Boss Bold is like lifting weights and building muscle: it takes time, dedication, and discipline. When you consistently command your thoughts in the right direction, it's incredible how empowered you will feel to move forward with the purpose God has put on your heart.

AFFIRMATIONS

I am creating my life by dominating my doubts and taking daily ACTION steps towards my ultimate life vision.

Other people and their opinions do not cause me to waver. I am a FORCE and I stand steadfast in my desire to fulfill my dreams.

> I am not only capable of pursuing my God-sized dreams, but I am equipped because my Creator has called me. I believe that past circumstances do not define my future reality. I am ready to step towards my future, and I am prepared and confident.

RESOURCES

1. *Hi God (It's Me Again)* by Nicole Crank
2. *Commanding Your Morning* by Cindy Trimm
3. *The Circle Maker: Praying Circles Around Your Biggest Dreams and Greatest Fears* by Mark Batterson

> You had a purpose
> before anyone had an opinion.
>
> #GoBossBold
> @LadyBoss_SP

CHAPTER 3

DARE TO JUMP

"You cannot just exist in this life. You have got to try to live. If you are waking up thinking there has got to be more to your life than there is, man, believe that it is. But to get to that life, you're gonna have to jump."
—Steve Harvey

Week 3

Tyler's Story

Tyler had a difficult childhood, to put it mildly. He grew up in an extremely abusive home with a violent father whose answer to everything was to "beat it out of him." He experienced sexual molestation at the hands of grown men on three different occasions and once by a friend's mother. So difficult was his early life that he attempted suicide as a child.

In the midst of the chaos, he was able to find moments of refuge when his mother would take him to church each week. He also found sanctuary in his thoughts and imagination. As a child, he constructed a "safe place" underneath the house porch made from wooden boards he had painted robin's egg blue. Here, he would let his imagination run free, and he would dream.

As Tyler grew older and left his childhood behind, unfortunately, the emotional scars followed him. However, one day in his early 20s, while watching The Oprah Winfrey Show, he took to heart the advice of one of the guests who suggested keeping a journal to help work out traumatic life events. He began writing a series of letters to himself, which he eventually would turn into his first musical, "I Know I've Been Changed."

Tyler dared to follow a dream as he invested the entirety of his savings to produce and release his musical to the public. However, it was poorly received and quickly became a financial failure—and thus began a period of massive testing of his faith. Over the next six years, he would face repeated box office failures, bad reviews, poverty, and even homelessness. Yet he persisted. He continually rewrote and retooled the musical, trying to perfect it for the audience, to no avail. Just as he was about to give up, he decided to put on one last show at the House of Blues in Atlanta, Georgia. It sold out. So did the next seven shows at that theater, and it continued to sell out as he moved it to larger and larger venues.

Tyler Perry's success with this musical led to a flood of new opportunities, including numerous plays, movies, and television shows. So prolific has his work been that, as of 2018, his estimated net worth was around $800 million.

"Sometimes when you follow God, things get tough, things get tight. But if you keep pushing, just on the other side of when you think it is the darkest, something miraculous will happen that will change your life. Something will open up that will blow your mind."

—Tyler Perry

"If you want to take the island you need to burn the boats."
—Tony Robbins

Tyler Perry's amazing story reinforces my belief that you are the only person in charge of what happens next in life. It's time to STOP procrastinating.

"It's not about choosing what you want right now. It is about choosing what you want most."
—Rachel Hollis

The more I coach, the more I see that fear is what holds most people from their God-sized dreams. As soon as things start to get uncomfortable, people tend to pull back, stop creating their lives, and return to default mode.

So, how do we deal with fear?

The following is a powerful way to stand strong against it.

BOSS BOLD POWER PRINCIPLE

Light your fears on FIRE

One of my favorite things to do in the wee hours of the morning is to sit out by the lake with a good book, an almond milk latte, and a fire crackling nearby in the outdoor fireplace. There's something almost magical about fire. Call me a little blonde arsonist, but I love tossing things in the fire and watching them get consumed by the flames.

It reminds me of the power of incinerating the things in our hearts and minds that don't serve our higher good. When we "let go, and let God," our fears are consumed by the flames of faith and disintegrate into a heap of ashes. With our fears gone up in smoke, there is nothing holding us back from our greatness. We can dare to JUMP, and when we do, anything is possible.

What fears do you need to send up in flames? Jot them down below!

_____

_____

_____

_____

Light your fears on FIRE

BOSS BOLD POWER PRINCIPLE

If I Fired My Fear Challenge

One of the ways I've been able to give back to the local community is by mentoring for the Minnesota Adult and Teen Challenge, a faith-based drug rehabilitation center in the Twin Cities. One weekend, I heard there was going to be a women's empowerment event taking place nearby, and I thought it sounded like just the thing that could make a difference in my mentee's life. Little did I know that I would be the one changed forever.

We arrived that day to a packed, standing-room-only arena, so we took our places up in the balcony. Each of the speeches were encouraging, enlightening, and helpful; however, one stood out to me in particular. It was delivered by an incredibly confident-appearing woman who, ironically, informed the audience that she had started off with no confidence. She went on to relate how she used faith to step out in courage anyway, despite her fear and anxiety. Then, she posed to us a life-altering question.

She passed out to each person in the audience a piece of paper that we were to fill out. The piece of paper asked us to complete a simple sentence: "If you fired your fear, you would <blank>." As soon as I read the question, the answer popped up in my mind automatically. I knew exactly what I'd do. Well, to be accurate, my heart knew, but my mind had doubts. The fears (doubts are fears), caused me to immediately retract within, and I didn't want to share my answer. So, I diverted to my mentee since I was there for her after all.

My mentee boldly shared hers, and I commended her for it. I assured her I would keep her accountable to her goal and would check in on her to make sure she was taking action. She thanked me and agreed, and I was relieved she hadn't asked mine.

If I Fired My Fear Challenge

Why didn't I want to share my answer? Honestly, I was afraid. I feared that if I shared it with her, she might laugh at how preposterous it was—or worse she might believe in me and hold me accountable. What if I failed? I'm the mentor here; I can't show her what failure looks like!

The speaker soon interrupted our conversation and my momentary relief as she commanded over the loudspeakers: "If you haven't shared your answer with your neighbor, do that now!" I had no choice. My mentee looked at me with bright eyes, excited to find out what I had written. I took a deep breath and told her, "Write a book."

I wanted to disappear. Who am I to write a book? I'm no author. I don't have the skills! And even if I did write a book, would anyone actually read it besides my mother? "That is amazing," she replied. "You are going to be an incredible best-selling author. You are going to change countless lives. You have already changed mine!" Then her tone changed from excitement to mild confusion. "Wait, why would YOU have fear around writing a book?"

I laughed sheepishly and proceeded to fill her in on the fears that were swirling in my head. She was stunned. She looked in my eyes and said, "Stef, that's what is so cool about you. I am surprised that you have any fears at all, but when you do have a fear, you step forward anyway and do what you set out to do. Thanks for being such an amazing example for me to follow."

Pretty sure the mentor/mentee relationship got flipped that night. Her words struck me, and that was the day I decided to set out on my journey to write a book. I dared to jump in spite of all the fears speaking their lies.

That night changed my life forever, and now, because I followed through on my dream, countless others are pursuing theirs.

BOSS BOLD
POWER MOVE

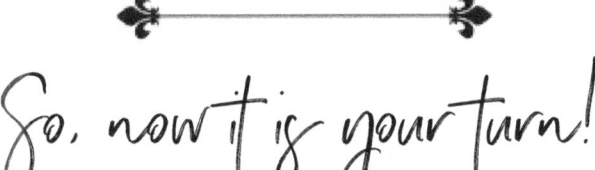

So, now it is your turn!

If I fired my fear, I would:
_____

Within 24 hours I will:
_____

My power partner to keep me accountable is: _____

> Put down this book, text your power partner right now, and tell that person what action you will take within the next 24 hours. Tell your partner you will text again in 24 hours and report what happened. Take a picture, post on Instagram, and tag me @LadyBoss_SP and hashtag #GoBossBold

BOSS BOLD POWER HABIT

Stefanie Peter's Power Habit:

It's extremely important to protect
your environment for growth!

Bold Boss Killers:

Distance yourself from doubters, haters, and the fearful. You can't reach the next level with negative energy pulling you backward.

Make a list of the Boss killers in your life (people, habits, lifestyle choices, and beliefs) and scratch one off your list every week until it's completely empty.

Take some time on the next page to journal your thoughts that are surfacing in this moment.

BOSS KILLERS

Never share big dreams with small-minded people!

1. Who are the people in my life that drain my energy? How can I put healthy boundaries in my life to protect myself or walk away?

　_____
　_____
　_____
　_____

2. What habits are no longer serving me and my higher self?

　_____
　_____
　_____
　_____

3. What lifestyle changes can I make to support my God-sized dream? Example: Exchange watching TV at night with working on one of my goals.

　_____
　_____
　_____
　_____

AFFIRMATIONS

I AM BOSS BOLD.
I am not shaken by fear.
I stand firm in the truth that
I am capable and qualified.

I AM brave, and I am responsible for my choices. I choose to go after my goals even when they seem like mountains.
I am unstoppable.

Write your own affirmation below:

_____
_____
_____
_____
_____

PRAYER

Father,

    Thank You for the vision and clarity that only You can provide. Your word tells me to "FEAR NOT" over and over again. So, today I ask that You link arms with me as I dare to jump and play all out for You. I pray that You move mountains, break chains, teach me how to fly, and be a soft place to land should I fall. Fill me with Your Holy Spirit. Challenge me to jump farther, and remind me that there is no distance that cannot be covered with You by my side.

Amen.

RESOURCES

1. *Jump: Take the Leap of Faith to Achieve Your Life of Abundance* by Steve Harvey
2. *Chase the Lion: If Your Dream Doesn't Scare You, It's Too Small* by Mark Batterson
3. *Dare to Dream and Work to Win: Understanding Dollars and Sense of Success in Network Marketing* by Dr. Tom Barrett

> A bigger game decision is the difference between an ordinary life and an extraordinary life.
>
> #GoBossBold
> @LadyBoss_SP

CHAPTER 4

BECOME A GOAL DIGGER

"Some people want it to happen, some wish it would happen, others make it happen."
—Michael Jordan

Week 4

Stevie's Story

Stevie came from a low-income family, wore hand-me-down clothing, and suffered from a stuttering problem. It didn't look like he had much going his way, but, still, he had a dream. He got a chance to reveal it one day in the sixth grade when his teacher gave the class an assignment to write down what they wanted to be when they grew up.

Stevie held nothing back. He had been inspired by a funny man he'd seen on television, and he knew he wanted to be on TV himself one day, making people laugh. He was proud of his dream and confidently wrote it down for the assignment.

The teacher reviewed the papers on the spot and began announcing to the class what each student had written down. When she got to Stevie's paper, however, she stopped and called him up to the front of the class. He was excited, anticipating what the teacher was going to say about him and his special dream.

To his surprise, the teacher asked sternly, "Why did you write that on your paper?"

"Because I want to be on TV!" he responded.

"Who do you know on TV? Anybody in this school ever been on TV?"

"No ma'am," he answered.

"Anyone in your family ever been on TV?"

"No ma'am."

"Then go home and write down something more realistic," she demanded.

Can you imagine how this would feel?

Stevie was devastated. He had never been so blatantly told what he could or couldn't do. He was beside himself as he told his father later that evening what had happened. His dad gave him some life-changing advice, though. He told Stevie to write down his dream and read it aloud morning and night, and thank God that one day he would be on TV.

Stevie did just that, year after year, until he realized his dreams. Today, you know this man as the great Steve Harvey, who makes people laugh every day with his own television show among other projects.

Steve said his dad taught him a major principle of success that day: "If you write it down and envision it, anything you see in your mind you can hold in your hand."

A humorous postscript to the story: Steve recently shared that every year for Christmas, he gifts that same teacher a new big-screen television so she can watch him making people laugh on the TV.

"Don't ever let someone tell you that you can't do something. Not even me. You got a dream, you gotta protect it. When people can't do something themselves, they're gonna tell you that you can't do it. You want something, go get it. Period."
--Will Smith
from Pursuit of Happyness

BOSS BOLD POWER PRINCIPLE

There are many lessons one could glean from observing the life and success of Steve Harvey, but one of the major themes that consistently arises is the power of "prayer and a pen." He wrote down his goal and thanked God constantly for it, and he saw it come to pass. Mark Batterson, one of my favorite authors, gives ten steps to setting life goals.

1. Start with prayer
2. Check your motives
3. Think in categories
4. Be specific
5. Write it down
6. Include others
7. Celebrate along the way
8. Dream big
9. Think long
10. Pray hard

BOSS BOLD POWER PRINCIPLE

QUESTION OF THE DAY:
DO YOU WANT TO MAKE TEN TIMES YOUR CURRENT INCOME?

Then set goals, Boss!

If you aren't yet convinced of the power of setting goals, perhaps this eye-opening study from Harvard will do the job.

In 1979, interviewers asked new graduates from Harvard's MBA program the following question: Have you set clear, written goals for your future and made plans to accomplish them? They found that:

- 84% had no specific goals at all
- 13% had goals but had not written them down
- 3% had written goals and plans to accomplish them

In 1989, the interviewers followed up with those same graduates and found some sobering results:

The 13% of the class who had unwritten goals were earning, on average, twice as much as the 84% who had no goals at all. Shockingly, the 3% who had clear, written goals were earning, on average, ten times as much as the other 97% combined.

BOSS BOLD POWER PRINCIPLE

So, are you starting to think it might be a good idea to write down your goals?

Let's go!

But FIRST:

1. PICK OUT YOUR WORD FOR THE YEAR!

Choose a single word to guide you for the new year, a single word that sums up the essence and focus for the next 365 days of your life. Having that guiding word changes everything. It allows you to step back and look at the big picture. What do you want to feel this year? What kind of experiences do you want to have? What results, effects, or changes do you want to see?

Example words: Joy, Faith, Impact, Intentional, Bold, Strong, Contribution

My word: _____

BOSS BOLD
POWER PRINCIPLE

2. CHOOSE YOUR POWER DECLARATION/SCRIPTURE!

Go to page 52 and write them below:

My Power Declaration/Scripture:

_____
_____
_____
_____
_____

BOSS BOLD
POWER PRINCIPLE

EXTRA CREDIT

PICK A SONG FOR THE YEAR THAT SETS YOUR SOUL ON FIRE!

This sets the tone for the year and empowers you to channel your inner Boss Bold self! I personally love to hit play and imagine my top ten goals becoming my reality. This is a powerful exercise to visualize your dream in full color and sink into all the feelings.

Some of my favorites: "Get Up" by Shinedown, "Come Alive" from *The Greatest Showman*, "Giants Fall" by Francesca Battistelli, "Miracle" by Unspoken, "Better When I'm Dancin'" by Meghan Trainor, "Brave" by Moriah Peters, "I Was Here" by Beyonce, "Confident" by Demi Lovato, just to name a few.

My song for the year:

_____

BOSS BOLD POWER MOVE

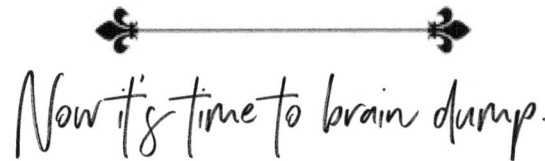

Now it's time to brain dump.

Fill out the answers to each category of goals and then highlight your top ten goals and write them out prioritized from 1 (being the most important) to the least important (on page 79)!

BUSINESS

(Examples: start a business, acquire a new skill, start a blog, write a book, take a social media course, delegate tasks, improve time management skills, grow to be number one in your industry, create a YouTube channel for your business, or build a creative team.)

1. _____

2. _____

3. _____

BOSS BOLD POWER MOVE

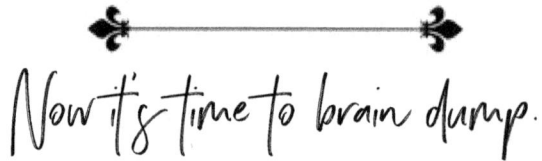

Now it's time to brain dump.

FINANCIAL

(Examples: get out of debt, pay off student loans, save for retirement, cut up credit cards, take a financial class, automate bill payment, buy a home, pay off a car loan, become financially independent, create multiple streams of residual income, or donate regularly.)

1. _____

2. _____

3. _____

PHYSICAL

(Examples: lose 15 pounds, eat healthier, work out daily, drink more water, schedule annual doctor appointments, start seeing a chiropractor, get a monthly massage, improve wardrobe, see a fashion consultant, improve physical appearance, see a hairstylist, take a new workout class, reduce sugar intake, or see a nutritionist.)

1. _____

2. _____

3. _____

BOSS BOLD POWER MOVE

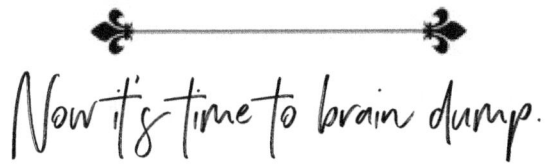

Now it's time to brain dump.

MENTAL

(Examples: read personal development books, take a course to expand your mind, get organized, make time for self-care, choose to be less stressed, choose to enjoy life, or choose to be happy and content while challenging your limits.)

1. _____

2. _____

3. _____

FAMILY

(Examples: create family fun days, find Mr./Ms. Right, send birthday cards/encouragement cards to close family/friends, plan a weekly date night, save for a dream vacation, or become a better mother/daughter/friend/girlfriend/wife/husband/son/boyfriend/father.)

1. _____

2. _____

3. _____

BOSS BOLD POWER MOVE

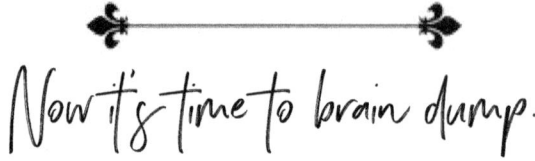

SPIRITUAL

(Examples: get involved in a group within church, do daily devotionals, volunteer, take a mission trip, donate to a non-profit, pray/meditate daily, or create a foundation to fund a cause.)

1. _____

2. _____

3. _____

LIFESTYLE

(Examples: take a cruise to the Greek Isles, take up a new hobby, start salsa lessons, redo your home office, travel to and speak at a leadership conference, attend a tech conference, host a book signing, meet a VIP, or visit Facebook headquarters.)

1. _____

2. _____

3. _____

BOSS BOLD POWER MOVE

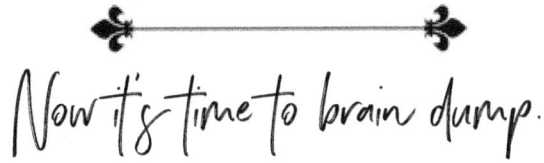

Now it's time to brain dump.

RELATIONSHIPS

(Examples: get a mentor, be a mentor, spend more time with friends, or cultivate and nurture relationships with like-minded achievers.)

1. _____

2. _____

3. _____

My Top Ten Prioritized Goals

1. _____ 6. _____

2. _____ 7. _____

3. _____ 8. _____

4. _____ 9. _____

5. _____ 10._____

BOSS BOLD POWER HABIT

Now that you have set your top ten goals for the year, prioritized your top three, and picked your word, mantra, or scripture for the year, it's time to create your power habit.

It's critical to be intentional and set the tone of your day FIRST thing in the morning. It's so easy to fall into the habit of jumping first thing onto social media, checking emails and texts and messages, and going down that whole time-consuming internet rabbit hole before your feet have even hit the floor. You are drained before you start your day and feel like you can never quite get it all together.

It's time for
The Thank You Card

THE THANK YOU CARD

This power habit alone has been a big game-changer for me. It puts me in peak state first thing in the morning, so I can run the day and the day doesn't run me.

Here's how it works. Take your word for the year, your power scripture/mantra, your top ten goals, and your affirmations, and use them to fill out a Thank You Card. I personally like to leave the gratitudes section blank so that I have to come up with new ones every day.

This is such a great way to organize these powerful tools in one place so you can master your morning all in one stop!

THE THANK YOU CARD

Here is the layout of the Thank You Card:
Feel free to fill it out here and then transfer it to a Thank You Card that you can take with you anywhere. DECLARE it EVERY morning to set the tone for each day!

My Word for the Year:

Scripture/Mantra

My Gratitudes
1. _____
2. _____
3. _____
4. _____
5. _____

Prayer of Thanks

My Top Ten Goals for the Year
10. _____
11. _____
12. _____
13. _____
14. _____
15. _____
16. _____
17. _____
18. _____
19. _____

My Affirmations

I am
I am
I am
I am
I am

AFFIRMATIONS

Today I have everything I need to succeed.

I am focused on positivity and productivity.

I am relentless. I am goal-oriented, and I concentrate my efforts on what I want to accomplish.

"Belief consists in accepting the affirmations of the soul; unbelief, in denying them."
—Ralph Waldo Emerson

PRAYER

Lord Jesus,

    You leave the 99 to pursue the one. Help me to set aside the things of this world so that I can pursue what You desire for me. Position my heart towards the goals that You have specifically designed for me. I no longer want to run in fear; instead I want fiercely to go after my God-sized dreams. I crave a relentless spirit, a spirit that boldly goes after divine direction. I pray Your Word inspires my steps and Your hand guides my goals. I invite You to fill any gaps, immerse me in Your love and favor, and help me to rise up for You.

Amen.

RESOURCES

1. *Goals!: How to Get Everything You Want—Faster Than You Ever Thought Possible* by Brian Tracy
2. *Living Your Best Year Ever: The Eight-Step Process for Achieving What You Want* by Darren Hardy
3. *Think and Grow Rich* by Napoleon Hill

> If you treat your business like a hobby it will
> pay you like a hobby....
> If you treat it like a business it will
> pay you like a business....
>
> #GoBossBold
> @LadyBoss_SP

CHAPTER 5

Chisel the Goal in Granite

Week 5

Louis' Story

Louis was born in Follansbee, West Virginia, in the cellar of the family home. The house had only one bedroom for his sister, himself, and his parents, and only a single half-bath with no tub, shower, or sink. He spent his early years in these humble beginnings, though many years later he'd say that he felt like he had been born with a silver spoon in his mouth, simply because he was born in a country with so much opportunity.

Eventually, Louis' family moved about 30 miles upriver to East Liverpool, Ohio. It was a small, simple town with only one high school, and high school football was everything. Louis' skill on the high school field led to him playing college ball as an undersized linebacker for Kent State University. Even though a knee injury would end his time as a player, he stuck with the sport and began coaching as an assistant for various teams.

The trajectory of his life seemed to slow, however, and six years into his career, he found himself an unemployed assistant football coach. To make matters more pressing, his wife was pregnant with their third child. Without an answer to his problems, he began to sink into discouragement.

His wife wasn't ready to give up, though, and began doing all she could to encourage him. In her attempts to lift him, she gave him the book *The Magic of Thinking Big*, by David J. Schwartz. It was this book that convinced Louis that if he wrote down his goals, he'd be able to achieve them. Inspiration hit him one night after reading the book, and he decided he was going to get out of his mental funk and change his life through setting and writing life goals.

He got to work and came up with a list of 107 crazy, larger-than-life goals that he intended to accomplish before he died. When he finished his list, his wife looked it over and said, "The list looks great, except you missed one. Get a job!"

Fortunately, the goals he wrote down would lead to many jobs, including being a successful head coach at six different colleges. Lou Holtz, as he's more commonly known, is perhaps best remembered for his tenure at the University of Notre Dame where, over 11 seasons, he led the Fighting Irish to nine consecutive bowl games and ended his career there with an overall record of 100 wins and only 30 losses. He's also written a number of books, had a successful career as a sports analyst and broadcaster, and even had a shot at coaching in the NFL.

As to the other things on his goal list, at last count he had achieved 102 out of 107, including having dinner at the White House with Ronald Reagan, cracking jokes on The Tonight Show with Johnny Carson, meeting the pope, parachuting out of an airplane, scoring a hole-in-one (two, actually), and becoming National Coach of the Year.

BOSS BOLD POWER PRINCIPLE

What an amazing example of the power of the pen and writing down your goals! If the past three life stories haven't convinced you of this yet, I'm not sure what will!

In the last chapter, I gave you the framework for brainstorming, organizing your goals, and then transferring them to an easy-reference, portable Thank You Card. Now we're going to go BIG using both words and images. I want to take your goal writing a step further and give you another powerful tool that works synergistically with the others. Today I'm going to walk you through creating a VISION BOARD.

I've used vision boards and goal posters for years, and they've been key to keeping my vision big and in the forefront of my mind at all times. Our minds think in both words and images, so it's incredibly powerful to combine both when it comes to keeping focused on our goals. Vision boards allow you to do just that.

Your vision board can be any size, but, personally, I like to go big. You can use any number of materials, including poster board, foam board, corkboard, or even flip charts. Really, any surface that you can write on, glue on, or attach things to should work. You can find these components at most office supply or arts and crafts stores.

There isn't necessarily a right or wrong way of crafting your vision board, so go as nuts with your creativity as you want. However, I found a way of organizing it that works best for me that might help you get started.

What I do is type out my top ten goals for the year, prioritize and number them from most important to least, and print them off. Then, I find images, either cut out from magazines or printed off the internet, that represent each goal. I then attach my goals in order to the board along with their corresponding pictures. Next to each goal, I write a desired deadline in pencil. I use pencil so that the deadline can easily be reset with just the swish of an eraser. Missing a deadline does not mean failure. What really counts is if you've gotten closer.

One final step I like to take is to print off my scripture and word for the year and attach them to the top of my board so I remember how I want to feel, who I want to impact, and why I am pursuing these goals. The vision board has proven to be a simple, yet powerful way of keeping my mind focused and aligned all year long.

BOSS BOLD POWER MOVE

Put together your vision board!

You can create it here or go all out at Hobby Lobby, buy a beautiful board, and make it an art piece. Either way works. Just make sure you do it as soon as possible. Remember, it doesn't need to be perfect for it to be effective.

YOUR VISION BOARD

YOUR VISION BOARD

BOSS BOLD POWER HABIT

Put your board somewhere you can't help but see it as you get ready for work in the morning and before bed at night. Spend at least five minutes each morning and night concentrating on the board and focusing on the feelings the words and images conjure within you. Use the board to help you visualize your goals in your mind's eye as reality. Don't forget to thank God for each one.

AFFIRMATIONS

I am exactly where I am supposed to be in this moment. I believe in myself. I am motivated and dedicated.

I am confident, fearless, and taking action today.

I am persistent and wise in my choices.

PRAYER

Father,

    Your word says that I am chosen and not forgotten. Today, I pray that You would continue to remind me of the passions and pursuits that You have chiseled into my heart. Thank You for preparing a path for me in this world. I pray that You strengthen every skill and talent needed to carry out Your plans for my life, but let me not forget to rely on You always. Lord, I pray that You would make me bold in my decisions and fearless in my actions. Thank You for Your gracious love and powerful Holy Spirit.

Amen.

RESOURCES

1. *Dream It. Pin It. Live It.: Make Vision Boards Work for You* by Terri Savelle Foy
2. *The Magic of Thinking Big* by David Schwartz
3. *Goal Setting* Audio Book by Jim Rohn

> Your mind must arrive at your destination before your life does.
>
> #GoBossBold
> @LadyBoss_SP

CHAPTER 6

Ignite Fearless Focus

"When you get focused on your dream, don't just drink the Kool-Aid. Swim in it. In other words, pour yourself into your dreams and become the best in your field."
—Grant Cardone

Week 6

Jasmine's Story

*"People think focus means saying yes to the thing you've got to focus on. But that's not what it means at all. It means saying no to the hundred other good ideas that there are. You have to pick carefully. I'm actually as proud of the things we haven't done as the things I have done.
Innovation is saying no to 1,000 things."*
—Steve Jobs

Jasmine, in her own assessment, wasn't much of a dreamer, even as a child—no playing dress up or planning dream weddings. As she got older, she tended to carefully adhere to the confines of what was safe and secure, which eventually led her to entering law school—a move she felt stifled her soul and extinguished the few dying embers of creativity she had. Fortunately, the right "spark" came along at the right time and reignited the dreams that had lain dormant all those years. The spark came in the form of a camera, which her husband gave her for Christmas one year.

She says she didn't realize it at the time, but as she was unwrapping that gift, she was unwrapping her dreams.

No more than four years after she made that decision, Jasmine had built a successful photography business, photographed hundreds of weddings, traveled the world, and been voted one of the "Top 10 Wedding Photographers in the World" by *American Photo* magazine. She credits letting her dreams steer her in life, rather than her fears.

BOSS BOLD
POWER PRINCIPLE

How does a Lady Boss with zero experience scale her business to one of the top ten wedding photographers in the world in an already saturated field?

One Word: FOCUS (pun intended)

There are so many elements of Jasmine Star's story that inspire me, but the one that strikes me most is how she ignited her own fearless focus to propel her to the top in less than four years.

Two major keys to maintaining focus are time management and prioritizing. It may come as a shock after all the emphasis I've put on taking action, but sometimes it's our busyness that keeps us from achieving our successful business. Sometimes our schedules are so full that they keep us distracted from focusing on the bigger picture and pursuing our real goals.

For some of us, the best thing we could do is take a bulldozer to our schedules. Many people who live by default rather than design fill their days with "urgent" but often unimportant activities, which eat up all their valuable time. Innocent things like emails, phone calls, social media, coffee dates, etc., can monopolize your time if not prioritized and properly managed.

"If you're going to risk and maybe fail, fail at something that matters. Fail gloriously so that even in failure, lives change."
—Jon Acuff

BOSS BOLD
POWER PRINCIPLE

These words may not sit well with you right now, but they are true. Your long-term goals are too important not to receive first priority, and they can't be cultivated in random five-minute increments here and there. You have to make ample space in your schedule to go after your goals and make your dreams reality.

Long-term goals need dedicated time. Uninterrupted time. Reserved time. And space. And more time. "Bliss-ipline!" Time stealers, while satisfying in the short term, often hijack your ability to set aside that much needed time and space. Time stealers also zap the energy and focus you need to pursue your long-term goals.

So how do you avoid the crazy, busy pitfall that we've all fallen into at one time or another? The answer is to learn the difference between your long-term goals and the trivial busyness of life. I'm going to teach you an important word today that you'll need to enter into your regular vocabulary.

That all-important word is "NO." It's a valid response. Don't be afraid to use it.

If your cell phone rings, dings, beeps, or buzzes while you're in the middle of a long-term goal project, don't answer it. "Deprioritize" the phone for later. A wrong-fit referral wants to "pick your brain" over coffee? Politely decline, or refer the contact to another professional. If you tend to fall victim to internet rabbit-hole syndrome, turn off your Wi-Fi until you've completed the important things. And so on. There are many ways to say "no" and many occasions that call for it. Long-term goals are all about saying "no" to the good so you can say "yes" to the great!

WHO ARE YOU?

Many people mistake "busy" for "productive" and feel they need to stay busy to feel worthy. "Stefanie, I need to do all these things on my to-do list!" With all due respect, "STOP the insanity!" Don't fear removing things from your calendar. Instead, fear investing in things that never really mattered in the first place.

	URGENT	NOT URGENT
IMPORTANT	**The Hot Mess** -Unscheduled rework -Last-minute changes -Daily fire-fighting -Micro-Managing	**The Boss** -Designing your dream life -Productive Collaborations -Creating creative content -Propelling your purpose forward
NOT IMPORTANT	**The Yes Mess** -Random interruptions -Babysitting your cousins best friend's daughter -Other people's emergencies	**The Rookie** -Mindless scrolling through Pinterest -Watching Netflix obsessively -Mall marathons -Major time stealers

HOW DO I ORGANIZE MY SCHEDULE?

Choose to live intentionally every day with your Dream Routine (DR) and Power Hours. Let's start with your Dream Routine (DR). When you start implementing your DR, you become the fabulous master of your day instead of a robot on autopilot pulled in a million different directions. Instead of impulsively checking your email when you wake up (which leads to putting out fire after fire), your DR will create a consistent routine that works for you.

My morning DR looks something like this:

1. Have my devotions, do some journaling, and read my Thank You Card (that includes my top goals for the year, my word and scripture for the year, affirmations, gratitude, and prayer). *See Chapter 4.
2. Exercise while listening to personal development topics via podcasts or the audible app on the phone. (Some of my personal favorites are Joel and Victoria Osteen, Nicole Crank, Joyce Meyer, Rebecca Jarvis, Craig Groeschel, Brendon Burchard, John Maxwell, Brian Tracy, Zig Ziglar, and Jim Rohn.)
3. Drink a green protein smoothie and take vitamins.

After your DR, it's time to implement your Power Hours. Power Hours are 55 minutes of uninterrupted time you spend laser-focusing on one of your long-term goals, followed by 5 minutes of rest. They are a must if you want to get to the next level. During your Power Hours, you're building, innovating, creating, and designing major aspirations, or using that time to grow or brainstorm your game plan with intention. Only after your DR and Power Hours should you begin your daily fire extinguishing.

Note: It's important that you find a DR and Power Hour method that works for you. I suggest the DR and Power Hours in the morning, but if you know you're a night person, consider having this time come later in the day or evening.

Research has shown that the brain absorbs information better when the learning is spaced out over time. As writer and entrepreneur Jenny Dearborn points out, if you don't change your scenery every now and then or take short breaks, your ability to learn and retain information will be impacted.

Duh! That impulse to check social media or grab a snack in the middle of a task is because your brain needs a break. The problem is that we don't have a game plan with breaks built-in. That's why I created the Power Hour for myself. Use a timer if you need to, and decide in advance not to allow any distractions. Period. Unless your workspace catches fire, you're in Boss Bold Fierce Focus mode.

I optimally like to conduct at least two Power Hours a day to complement my three non-negotiable goals for the week. Pick how many Power Hours you can realistically commit to for the week, and block out time for those so you can propel your top three goals forward.

For example: Let's say one of your top three goals for the quarter is to complete the online course you purchased to move your business forward. So, take out your calendar and block off two Power Hours for the week—maybe one on Monday from noon to 1 p.m. and one for Wednesday at the same time of day. When those days and times arrive, set your timer on your phone for 55 minutes, turn your phone to airplane mode if need be so you don't get distracted, and dive into the online course. Then, when the timer dings, get up and do some jumping jacks to revitalize you, and dive into another Power Hours or get on with your day!

You will be AMAZED at how much you can get done in focused bursts of time versus getting distracted by every text, email ping, phone call, or side advertisement on your computer calling your name with a flash sale. Don't get me wrong, I love a flash sale, but I will reward myself with that after I have moved a goal forward.

Power Hours ensure that I make progress daily on what I know I need to get done—no ifs, ands, or putting a goal on the backburner. This practice takes crazy discipline. But you know what? Discipline is the key to becoming successful.

Another crucial way to keep yourself fiercely focused and your feet to the fire is finding a power partner. A fellow go-getter in your corner challenging you regularly and checking in on your progress is one of the most fabulous strategies for crossing the finish line.

BOSS BOLD
POWER MOVE

My fearless focus power plan

Create your DR (Dream Routine) and stick to it for a week. Evaluate how it transforms your mindset, and observe how it helps your productivity. What are three things that you can do daily to set your day up for success and have you feeling fabulous?

My Dream Routine to set me up for success daily:

_____

_____

_____

My Top Three Goals

_____

_____

_____

BOSS BOLD
POWER HABIT

Power Hours are the key to propelling my goals and dreams into reality.

I will conduct _____ Power Hours this week to move my top three goals forward!

GOAL # 1:

_____

POWER HOURS THIS WEEK:

_____

_____

GOAL #2:

_____

POWER HOURS THIS WEEK:

_____

_____

BOSS BOLD POWER HABIT

Power Hours this week

GOAL #3:

_____

POWER HOURS THIS WEEK:

_____
_____

Three things I will STOP doing to give me more time to work on my goals:

1. _____

2. _____

3. _____

BOSS BOLD POWER MOVE

In order to achieve your goals, you need to break down the big goal into bold action steps. That's where the "Boss Bold Moves" come in! Example: Let's say you want to write a book. I would break that down into the first three "Boss Bold Moves" with deadlines.

Now it's your turn! Take your top three goals and break them down with action steps and deadlines:

Goal 1:   To be completed by:

1ST BOSS BOLD MOVE: _____

2ND BOSS BOLD MOVE: _____

3RD BOSS BOLD MOVE: _____

Goal 2:   To be completed by:

1ST BOSS BOLD MOVE: _____

2ND BOSS BOLD MOVE: _____

3RD BOSS BOLD MOVE: _____

Goal 3:   To be completed by:

1ST BOSS BOLD MOVE: _____

2ND BOSS BOLD MOVE: _____

3RD BOSS BOLD MOVE: _____

AFFIRMATIONS

I am in command of my life. I don't let my emotions dictate my plan. I let my vision drive my actions.

I am fully present. I am taking bold steps and moving forward with confidence.

I am a born leader. I am successful because I stay focused on my goals and God-sized dream.

PRAYER

Lord,

    Thank You for showing me that as long as my confidence is rooted and grounded in You, there is nothing to fear. You have the power. You go before me, and You walk beside me. I pray that You stay close and present. Jesus, thank You for equipping and empowering me to face any mountain or storm that comes my way. I declare that I am fearless because of Your faithfulness.

Amen.

RESOURCES

1. *The Power of Focus* by Mark Victor Hansen
2. *The Miracle Morning: The 6 Habits That Will Transform Your Life Before 8AM* by Hal Elrod
3. *Eat That Frog! 21 Great Ways to Stop Procrastinating and Get More Done in Less Time* by Brian Tracy

> If getting up 30 minutes earlier to pursue your God-sized dream seems overwhelming, you've either got the wrong dream or you're just pretending you have one... #BOSSUP
>
> #GoBossBold
> @LadyBoss_SP

CHAPTER 7

FAIL FAST & FURIOUS

"The less you venture out, the greater your risk of failure. Ironically the more you risk failure—and actually fail—the greater your chances of success."
—John C. Maxwell

Week 7

Mr. Washington's Story

"I was flunking out of college. I had a 1.7 grade point average. I hope none of you can relate. I was sitting in my mother's beauty parlor, and I was looking in the mirror, and I saw behind me this woman under the dryer, and every time she looked up, every time I looked up, she was looking at me, just looking me in the eye. I didn't know who she was. She said, 'Somebody get me a pen, get me a pencil, I have a prophecy.' March 27, 1975, she said,

> *'Boy, you are going to travel the world and speak to millions of people.'*

"Now mind you, I flunked out of college. I'm thinking about joining the army. I didn't know what I was going to do, and she's telling me I'm going to travel the world and speak to millions of people. Well, I have traveled the world and I have spoken to millions of people. That's not the most important thing—the success that I've had. The most important thing is that what she taught me and what she told me that day has stayed with me since. I've been protected, I've been directed, I've been corrected. Fail BIG. That's right. Fail BIG. You only live once, so do what you feel passionate about.

Take chances professionally; don't be afraid to fail. There's an old IQ test with nine dots and you had to draw five lines with a pencil within these nine dots without lifting the pencil. The only way to do it was to go outside the box. So, don't be afraid to go outside the box. Don't be afraid to think outside the box. Don't be afraid to fail big, to dream big."

Mr. Washington's Story

This man, who seemed to be starting out life on a failing path, is better known as the award-winning actor and producer, Denzel Washington.

His life is testament to the fact that your start doesn't define your finish, nor do your past failures define your future.

At the beginning of my career, I wanted everything to be perfect. I made the mistake of becoming consumed by an idealized image of how I wanted to be, rather than embracing who I already was. Over time, my perfectionism became paralyzing. I couldn't make a move unless I knew it would turn out flawlessly.

You can imagine how much I got done in those early days—not much. But then I read *Failing Forward* by John C. Maxwell, and something clicked. It was a life-changer. For the first time, I felt I had permission to fall flat on my face and still come out a champion in the end. His advice helped take the pressure off, and it gave me not only the freedom to fail but also a sense of urgency to "fail fast." I learned that if I failed fast, I could more quickly figure out what worked and what didn't.

It may sound counter-intuitive, but failure is a necessary step on the way to success. And it's unavoidable. You'll never achieve success without it. In fact, the more failures I experience, the more success I have. When I first began learning to run my business, I had to fail often, because if I wasn't failing, I wasn't trying enough new things. Lack of failure means you're not playing a big enough game; you're being way too cautious.

SOMETIMES YOU WIN SOMETIMES YOU LEARN

I get it: Failure sucks. Who doesn't hate failing? But it sucks far less when you accept that it's a normal and necessary part of success. And I don't believe we ever truly have to fail, in the sense that failure is often mistakenly equated to "losing." The title of one of Maxwell's books says it perfectly: *Sometimes You Win, Sometimes You Learn.*

The only way to lose is not to learn from your failures. Either we win or we learn. And Lord knows I have learned a lot along the journey.

When you begin to view your failures as learning opportunities, you begin to see them for what they are: the start of something spectacular. Every Boss—from Arianna Huffington (founder of *Huffington Post*) to Joyce Meyer (world-renowned evangelist) to Tina Fey (comedic goddess), have epic failure stories. In my last book I related the story of Sara Blakely, the founder of Spanx. She has one of the most spectacular failure-to-fortune stories ever. If you haven't read it, it's worth checking out. The Fail Fast and Furious Club is one all Bosses join, whether we like it or not.

"When your goal is to gain experience, perspective, and knowledge, failure is no longer a possibility."
—Sophia Amoruso, author of #girlboss and founder of nasty gal

---

FAILING FORWARD

On the very first page of this workbook, I promised I'd share the story of how I struck out with one sponsor before hitting a home run with Calvin Klein, Fabletics, and some other amazing brands. So, here goes.

It was the summer before my first book was going to be published, and I was envisioning my ultimate book launch. I wanted to create an unforgettable experience that would inspire women and encourage them to follow their dreams. But I also wanted something fabulous that my fellow Boss Babes would love that reflected our energy and style.

So, naturally, I came up with ... a fashion show between giant speakers! What else? I was so excited about my idea. I grabbed pen and paper and began writing down my ideal sponsors. I decided on Victoria's Secret, Calvin Klein, Fabletics, Mainstream Boutique, and some type of makeup sponsor.

However, it hit me pretty quickly that I had absolutely zero connections to most companies. After thinking it over for a bit, I decided I'd just have to make my own connections by showing up to their stores and asking. So, I prepared a pitch, grabbed some business cards, and set off to share the vision.

First stop, Victoria's Secret. I asked for a manager and once she arrived (after a strangely long wait), I gave her my pitch. I told her that I was hosting a book launch there at the Mall of America, and I described how their participation could help us both. I explained that women were coming to the event from all over the country, that there would be powerhouse speakers, and the fashion show would be a phenomenal way to drive traffic to their store. Therefore, it could be a great marketing opportunity to boost holiday sales.

FAILING FORWARD

Her response: "We have the angels and would not be interested in participating on any level."

Oh, I'm sorry. You have the angels? Well, maybe you and your precious "angels" would instead like to kiss my shiny, white ... but, yeah, I didn't really say that.

I thanked her and walked out of the store feeling deflated. That certainly wasn't what I had expected. There was definitely an opportunity to take that rejection as a sign that it was all going to fail and I should give up. But I thought to myself: They weren't a sponsor before I walked in, and they aren't a sponsor now. Nothing changed except maybe a bit of a bruised ego. Who cares?

Onward and upward! I walked into the next store, Calvin Klein. I gave my same spiel and braced for impact. But this time the manager had a completely different reaction. The manager, Angie, said they had never done anything like this before, but she wanted to call corporate to see what they could do and that she'd get back to me. I thanked her for her time and walked out thinking no matter what the verdict, I was proud that I kept going even after the first loud "no."

Angie texted me back three hours later and said they would provide more than half the outfits for the fashion show and donate water bottles in every Lady Boss swag bag at the event! I was elated. Then, Fabletics and Mainstream Boutique jumped on board too. I couldn't help but think, what if I would have stopped at Victoria's Secret and let the first "fail" take me down?

If failures are learning points, that "fail" taught me not to give up.

OTHER EPIC FAILURES

Vera Wang failed to make the U.S. Olympic figure skating team. Afterward she went into the fashion industry and became an editor at *Vogue*. She began designing wedding gowns at age 40, created her own fashion label, and today she is valued at over $650 million.

Tim Ferriss had 26 publishing rejections for his book, *The 4-Hour Workweek*, before it ended up on *The New York Times* Bestseller list.

Arianna Huffington's first book was well-received, but her second book was rejected by 36 publishers. She has since written 13 books and become a successful journalist and entrepreneur.

Lisa Kudrow was originally offered the role of Roz on the television show, "Frasier," but after two rehearsals the showrunners decided she wasn't a good fit and let her go. She went on to play Phoebe on one of the most successful sitcoms of all time, "Friends," along with other television and movie roles.

Brian Acton dreamed of working at Facebook or Twitter. After an interview with Twitter, he tweeted, "Got denied by Twitter HQ. That's ok. Would have been a long commute." He then landed an interview with Facebook, after which he announced: "Facebook turned me down. It was a great opportunity to connect with some fantastic people. Looking forward to life's next adventure." But instead of giving up, he got creative. He teamed up with a co-worker from his job at Yahoo and created the app called WhatsApp, which he sold to Facebook for $19 billion five years later.

Let success be a marathon, not a sprint.

BOSS BOLD
POWER PRINCIPLE

What is a recent failure you had? Recall and write the lessons you learned from it. Make sure not to fall into a pity party or hold resentments when you do this exercise. List three ways you intend to turn your failure into a win for your playbook.

1. _____

2. _____

3. _____

Encourage another Boss who you know is struggling with failure. Remind them that you only fail if you quit. Suggest a baby step they can take right now to keep them moving forward.

Create a Fail Forward Action Plan. What are you going to do to rebound from your recent failure? Who in your tribe can help you bridge the gap? What can you do right now to meaningfully move forward?

___

FAIL FASTER
SUCCEED FASTER

You may be just one "no" away from an epic "YES," so, let's get this party started!

The quicker you find out what doesn't work, the quicker you can figure out what does.

Asking for the sale, the date, the interview, the promotion can be intimidating.

It's almost as if we are programmed to take rejection personally.

Our minds tell us that it is our very personhood being rejected. But that's not it at all. When someone says "no," they are simply saying "no" to that specific offer, at that specific time.

So, let's change that mindset.

When we understand that "no" is a part of life and is what will get us closer to success, we will see the value in it and move forward faster.

BOSS BOLD POWER MOVE

Think of ten people from whom you could request something. But here's the thing: Think of requests to which they'll probably say "no."

Since you'll be expecting, even wanting, to receive the "no," it takes all the fear out of receiving it. This exercise will help your mind get used to what it feels like not to fear that dreaded little two-letter response.

Make the list, make the asks, and go for NO. Play the game and have FUN with it!

1. _____
2. _____
3. _____
4. _____
5. _____
6. _____
7. _____
8. _____
9. _____
10. _____

Extra Credit: Make a list of 100 people you will ask within the month!

BOSS BOLD
POWER HABIT

There are some obstacles you can't anticipate or remove completely. When they come along, stop, pray, and ask God how to navigate around them. Trust God to lead you through.

If He has purposed for you to do something, *He will make a way! Nothing can stop His plan for your life.*

If you think you've blown God's plan for your life, rest in this: You, my beautiful friend, are not that powerful.

AFFIRMATIONS

Failing is not final ... it is my stepping stone to success.

Either I win or I learn ... I never lose unless I refuse to "learn" from the failure.

I fail regularly, therefore I am unstoppable.

PRAYER

Lord,

Thank You for infusing my spirit with Your wisdom. Thank You for Your guidance and daily reminders that I am pushing forward for a purpose and in Your purpose. I pray for Your strength and tenacity as I move forward in building the calling that You have placed on my heart. I humbly ask that You walk before me, carve out my path, and remind me that when I fall, I am not a failure. Thank You for Your loving grace, for allowing me to be a part of Your plan, and for seeing me through every storm that I will encounter on this journey. Walk beside me, O Lord, and light my path. In Your precious name, Jesus.

Amen.

RESOURCES

1. *Failing Forward: Turning Mistakes into Stepping Stones for Success* by John C. Maxwell
2. *If: Trading Your If Only Regrets for God's What If Possibilities* by Mark Batterson
3. *It's Not Over Until You Win: How to Become the Person You Always Wanted To Be No Matter What the Obstacle* by Les Brown

> People are impressed by your success, but impacted by your failure... My two cents: Fail fast and furious to inspire the masses to greatness!
> #GoBossBold @LadyBoss_SP

CHAPTER 8

MASTER YOUR MINDSET

"No matter what, people grow. If you chose not to grow, you're staying in a small box with a small mindset. People who win go outside of that box. It's very simple when you look at it."
—Kevin Hart

Week 8

Tim's Story

"Success is not to be pursued; it is to be attracted by the person you become."
—Jim Rohn

I'll just jump right in and let you know that this story is about Tim Tebow, whose inspirational story is still unfolding before the public's eyes even right now. He faces highs and lows, failures and successes, seemingly month by month, and he always does it with grace and a great attitude.

You might remember Tim as the super college athlete who won both the Heisman Trophy and the BCS National Championship while playing for the Florida Gators. You might remember him for pulling off amazing come-from-behind victories once he got to the NFL, and still being cut from teams. In fact, he's the only quarterback in NFL history to have won a playoff game and then never started another game. In 2016, Tim began to pursue a career in professional baseball instead, where he has continued to ride the rollercoaster of successes and seeming failures. Fans of Tim Tebow have every reason to see him as a major success, even though the highs and lows of life have had him playing offense and defense.

But not everyone is a fan of Tim Tebow. Recently, an interviewer sat down with the now baseball player and came right out and said, "I've read that you're a farce. I've read that you're a joke. I've read that you're an embarrassment—not only to yourself but to the game of baseball."

Tebow calmly responded in a masterful way. He said: "The first thing is, I'm so thankful that I don't have to read it. I don't have to listen to it. I don't have to live the rollercoaster that the rest of the world lives of my life."

Tim's Story

"I don't care what they write about me. And they've written a lot of things over the last 15 years about me: some good, some not good, some just because they want to sell papers. I don't necessarily care. At the end of the day, I want to pursue my passion because I believe when you're pursuing what's on your heart, when you're pursuing what you're convicted by, then I don't have to live with regret 10-15-20 years from now, looking back saying, 'What if? What if I would have tried that?'"

Preach it, Tebow! I don't know if I would have responded so calmly to such a nasty interviewer. But the more I live life, the more I realize how important it is to stay mentally tough and in the game if you truly want to accomplish the dream God has placed on your heart.

THE ONLY THING STANDING BETWEEN YOU AND YOUR GOALS ARE THE BS STORIES YOU TELL YOURSELF AND THE LYING VOICES YOU LISTEN TO.

In his book, *Shaken*, Tim Tebow talks about how he handles the highs and lows as they come:

"Was my identity found in those highs when we were making a playoff run? No. Was my identity found a year later when I was being let go? No. I was excited, proud, happy, disappointed, and sad at times, but that's not what made me—that's not who I was and that's not who I am."

THE WORLD DOESN'T GET TO DEFINE YOU BECAUSE GOD ALREADY DID THAT.

I go into great depth on how to "Master Your Mindset" in my book *Unleash Your Lady Boss*, so if you want to get the nitty-gritty details you should definitely snag that resource. But I'll outline a few of the highlights here as well as some extra tips I have learned since then.

BOSS BOLD
POWER PRINCIPLE

First, I'll let you know that mastering your mindset can be one of the most exhilarating and empowering things you can do for yourself and the people around you. It may not be easy, but once you master it there are no limits to what you can accomplish.

There's a reason I started this chapter with the story of an athlete. I see so many parallels between manifesting a "game mindset" and mastering your mindset for a successful life. And the inspirational stories we can find in the sports world apply so aptly to our own lives as we make our journey and face our own giants.

Now, this may be cheating a little because he isn't a real athlete, but I love what Sylvester Stallone's character, Rocky, has to say about facing challenges.

> "Let me tell you something you already know. The world ain't all sunshine and rainbows. It is a very mean and nasty place. And it will beat you to your knees and keep you there permanently if you let it. You, me, or nobody is gonna hit as hard as life. But it ain't how hard you hit; it's about how hard you can get hit, and keep moving forward. How much you can take, and keep moving forward. That's how winning is done. Now, if you know what you're worth, then go out and get what you're worth. But you gotta be willing to take the hit, and not pointing fingers saying you ain't where you are because of him, or her, or anybody. Cowards do that and that ain't you. You're better than that."

BOSS BOLD POWER PRINCIPLE

In life when we face challenges, we have two choices: run away in fear, or rise up in faith and let God move mountains on our behalf. When mastering your mindset, just like in sports, I believe you need to play solid offense and defense.

DEFENSE: The action of defending from or resisting attack
OFFENSE: The action of attacking

You need to focus on attacking life head-on, but also know how to defend yourself when something (I call it life) happens.

This section is dedicated to learning how to "Boss up," break out of your rut, and move into massive momentum.

A Boss that is going to do BIG things cannot let small things get to them! Ask yourself, is this going to matter a year from now? If not, let that shit go … Your energy is your currency.

POWER QUOTES

The lie—I need a hero.
The truth—I need to become my own hero.

Stop waiting for someone else to change the game for you.

Comfort and convenience run the lives of unsuccessful people.
#BossUp

Part of life is finding your comfort zone and staying out of it!

You've always had the power,
it's just a matter of stepping into your power every single day!

And last, but not least this is from one of my favorite preachers:
"Leadership rises and falls on your ability to handle pressure."
—Pastor David Crank

FAITH OR FIXED

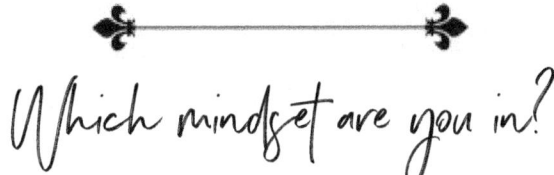

Which mindset are you in?

FIXED MINDSET	FAITH MINDSET
1) Avoid challenges	1) Embrace challenges
2) Give up easily due to obstacles	2) Persist despite obstacles
3) See efforts as fruitless	3) See effort as a pathway to mastery
4) Be Threatened by others' success	4) Be Inspired by others' success
5) Stay stuck in a problem	5) Figure out a solution
6) Settle for the status quo	6) Constantly challenge the status quo
7) Hate change	7) Disrupt an industry and thrives on innovation
Example: I am worthless when it comes to technology.	Example: YouTube is my friend, and I am willing to learn technology.
Example: That girl/guy on Instagram has it all together. I don't have what it takes.	Example: That girl/guy on Instagram has it all together. That's my cue that I can too.

PERSONAL GROWTH PLAN

I believe you are the sum average of your five closest friends, the books you read, the places you go, and the podcasts you listen to. Choose them wisely!

> *Here's the way I view it: life is a personal development plan with a pay plan attached.*

I got some flack when I posted this on Facebook, but I will say it again since I think I owe it to my friends to speak the truth: My two cents: Don't take financial advice from a person who is broke.

Success leaves clues. Don't get me wrong; money definitely isn't everything, but it gives you options, freedom, and the opportunity to affect other's lives. Who in your life is leaving clues? How can you learn from them and implement those principles in your life?

_____
_____
_____
_____
_____
_____

PERSONAL GROWTH PLAN

THE FOLLOWING LIST CAME FROM TOM CORLEY'S BOOK, *RICH HABITS.*
THESE ARE 16 HABITS OF THE RICH:

1.	Eat Healthy	70% of wealthy eat less than 300 junk food calories per day. 97% of poor eat more than 300 junk food calories per day.
2.	Focus	80% of wealthy are focused on accomplishing a single goal. Only 12% of poor do this.
3.	Exercise	76% of wealthy exercise aerobically four days a week. 23% of poor do this.
4.	Listen	63% of wealthy listen to audiobooks during commute to work vs. 5% for poor people.
5.	To-Do	81% of wealthy maintain a to-do list vs. 19% of poor.
6.	Call	80% of wealthy make HBD (Happy Birthday Calls) vs. 11% of poor.
7.	Write Goals	67% of wealthy write down their goals vs. 17% for poor.
8.	Read	88% of wealthy read 30 minutes or more each day for education or career reasons vs. 2% for poor.
9.	Speak Your Mind	6% wealthy say what's on their mind vs. 69% for poor.
10.	Network	79% of wealthy network five hours or more each month vs. 16% for poor.
11.	Less TV	67% of wealthy watch one hour or less of TV every day vs. 23% for poor.
12.	No Trash TV	6% of wealthy watch reality TV vs. 78% for poor.
13.	Rise Early	44% of wealthy wake up three hours before work starts vs. 3% for poor.
14.	Improve and Learn	86% of wealthy believe in life-long educational self-improvement vs. 5% for poor.
15.	Avoid Toxic People	86% of wealthy associate with other successful people. 96% of poor associate with others who are poor.
16.	Don't Give Up	Wealthy have three things in common: focus, persistence, and patience. They simply do not quit chasing their big goals. Those who struggle financially stop short.

IT'S TIME TO GO PRO

There is not a single, "right" way of approaching life. I respect all different types of people from all different backgrounds. But I just want to make sure that if you choose a path of dreaming big, you understand what it takes to get there! I've worked with too many people who felt as if they were born to do something amazing but had no clue how to get there or even where to begin. Achieving big dreams requires a game plan and a strategy. Hope is not a strategy. We need to become aware of what is required and then craft a plan to close the gaps and get after it.

    I love to break my personal growth plan into quarters for the year. It gives me a quick snapshot and visual of where I am going, what I am doing, and the goals I am pursuing with a simple breakdown to keep my eye on my priorities.

You are either growing or dying.

GO PRO PERSONAL DEVELOPMENT PLAN

Listed below are the questions I ask myself so I know what I need to pursue to go pro!

1. What is the one thing that, if mastered, would make everything else I do easier or unnecessary?

    _____

2. How can I become an expert in my industry or profession?

    _____

3. How can I increase my service?

    _____

4. What type of person do I need to become in order to accomplish my dream?

    _____

5. What skill am I missing and need to master?

    _____

6. There are always better ways to do what I'm presently doing. What are they?

    _____

7. How will my work be performed 20 years from now?

    _____

GO PRO PERSONAL DEVELOPMENT PLAN

This next set of questions will give you a solid game plan to up-level your life and create the infrastructure for personal development! Once you are finished you can fill out the chart and be confident in your strategy for growth.

1. Which books will empower me to master the "one thing" I listed on the previous page? Which books will equip me to make an impact? Which books will challenge me to "Boss up?" How many books do I want to read a year?

_____
_____
_____

2. Which events do I need to attend to sharpen my "blade"? How many events do I want to attend per year? (I recommend attending an event or online course every quarter.)

_____
_____
_____

3. What type of a coach do I need to hire to take my business to that next level? Pro Tip: Interview at least three coaches and make sure they have the credibility and skills to get you where you want to go (just speaking from experience).

_____
_____
_____

GO PRO PERSONAL DEVELOPMENT PLAN

4. What type of mastermind group do I need to create or attend to expand my point of view and grow as a leader?

_____
_____
_____

5. What collaboration(s) do I need to create to soar to new heights with like-minded Bosses?

_____
_____
_____

6. What type of class(es) do I need to attend to up-level my skills?

_____
_____
_____

BOSS BOLD
POWER HABIT

These are a lot of deep questions to answer, but you can be selective and choose the ones that apply best, based on what you want to do and where you want to go. I recommend asking these questions quarterly and implementing what applies.

If you are new to the personal development game, and you haven't read a book since college, don't worry. Buy one book and commit to reading just ten pages before you go to work or before bed at night. Then repeat.

"Don't be too hard on yourself, but don't let yourself off the hook."

This month I will read the book:

_____

_____

_____

_____

BOSS BOLD
POWER MOVE

My Word for the Year:

My Scripture/Mantra for the Year:

January – March	
Books I will read:	
Events I will attend:	
Courses I will take:	

April - June	
Books I will read:	
Events I will attend:	
Courses I will take:	

July - September	
Books I will read:	
Events I will attend:	
Courses I will take:	

October - December	
Books I will read:	
Events I will attend:	
Courses I will take:	

AFFIRMATIONS

I have a mindset of ABUNDANCE!

I attract God-sized ideas that create great wealth!

_____

PRAYER

Father,

    Thank You for providing me with Your Word. Thank You for pouring Your Holy Spirit abundantly and for renewing my mind when I call upon You. You are my revival, and because of that, I know I can master my mindset and keep my heart postured toward You and Your will for my life.

Amen.

RESOURCES

1. *Shaken: Discovering Your True Identity in the Midst of Life's Storms* by Tim Tebow
2. *Battlefield of the Mind* by Joyce Meyer
3. *The Success Principles* by Jack Canfield

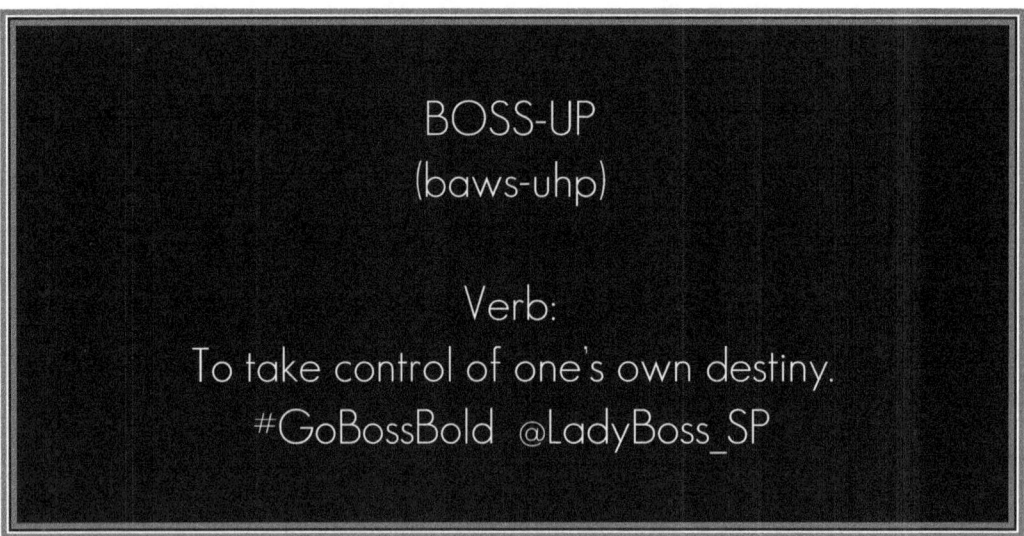

CHAPTER 9

BUILD YOUR DREAM TRIBE

"Some people will hear you louder in silence. Those are your tribe—they'll get you through the tough days and give you something to laugh about on the ride."
—Nikki Rowe

Week 9

Emily's Story

Emily Frisella grew up on a crop and cattle farm in small-town Missouri. Her knowledge of agriculture led her to open her first business, a flower shop with home-grown products, at age 20. Even though she eventually sold her business and moved to the big city, her business acumen followed her. She was passionate about health and had loved cooking from a young age, but she noticed so many recipes required exotic or expensive ingredients. Why couldn't they just use stuff that most people either already had in their kitchens or were easy to find at the local grocery store? So she said, "Screw this! I'm writing my own cookbooks for real people!"

She started a blog and a Facebook page that featured her own creative recipes and began to create a following. She knew she could make her brand fly if she nurtured a tribe and showed up to make it happen every day online. She worked nights and weekends committing to her brand, business, and followers, and was able to leave her job within two years. Emily essentially built her entire business online, and her "Fit Home & Health" brand is thriving! Talk about the power of Wi-Fi and a dream.

I met this phenomenal Lady Boss when I was launching my first book, as we had the same publisher. I was amazed at the amount of love and support she received when she launched her cookbook. But as I got to know her, it was no surprise as to why she had such a strong launch. This Boss Babe is the real deal, and she knows how to build a rock-solid tribe.

She puts in a ton of sweat equity and truly cares about those she is impacting. That's why I wanted to share her story and the insights she shared with me on how to build your ultimate Boss tribe!

Thanks, Emily, for blazing the trail!

Emily's Story

Emily's top three tips on how to cultivate your ultimate culture, community, and dream tribe:

Being an entrepreneur is not for the faint of heart, but Emily has built an incredibly loyal following by putting in the time and taking care of her audience. She has a phenomenal following that not only "likes" her photos, but also engages with her and her content. Her brand has evolved into lifestyle, motivation, and inspiration. Through this shift, Emily has created brand ambassador programs, partnered with other influencers, been hired by big brands, and advised wealth-management company owners, attorneys, authors, doctors, and many others.

I share all this to say: Your dream requires hard work, hustle, and heart. But a tribe is what ignites the spark! Building your dream tribe takes some serious effort, but I believe it is what shifts things from success to significance and making a major impact in the marketplace.

P.S. Here is my plug for this beautiful soul, Emily! If you are looking to get inspired and take some tips from a pro, follow her @EmilyFrisella on Instagram!

Emily's top three tips on how to cultivate your ultimate culture, community, and dream tribe:
- Take advantage of the free platform of social media and connect on a heart level.
- Give valuable and inspirational content no matter how big or small your following; it builds major "know, like, and trust," and will eventually ignite as you put out consistent content.
- Add value by commenting back on your people's posts, and take interest in them!

BOSS BOLD PRINCIPLE

Building your dream tribe can be a blast, but there will be bumps along the way! It can be a little challenging finding your A-team, but just know you have two options: 1) Say, "This is as good as it gets" and stay stagnant within your current circle, or 2) Draw a line in the sand, and make it your mission to develop your ultimate Boss tribe!

"It's critical to seek out like-minded, purpose-driven individuals whose mission falls into alignment with yours."
—Stefanie Peters

As you inch closer to the life you've always dreamed of building, you'll realize that your tribe is the missing link. They are the individuals who energize, motivate, push you, and ultimately embrace your potential and vision.

Look at your goals—past, present, and future. Where do you want to be in the next year, five years, or even ten years?

Be intentional when selecting your tribe. Diversity is key. When you have a dynamic mixture of people from all walks of life, you'll find that each person comes to the table with different strengths. As a collective, these strengths are magnified, and your team is able to accomplish exponentially more than any one person on their own.

BOSS BOLD PRIMCIPLE

"One can chase a thousand, and two shall put ten thousand to flight."
—Joshua 23:10

Write down what your ultimate tribe looks like. Are you lacking sales savvy? Financial prowess?

Do you need a good referral partner? What about a prayer partner or workout buddy? Your tribe isn't all about business all the time. Your tribe is poised to bolster your life goals, and that includes the whole shebang: family, spiritual, creative, and financial goals. And that's why it's crucial that you remove toxic folks from the mix. Yep, I'm going there. Bosses, if you want to go after your life's next chapter in a major way, you need to evaluate the people who are influencing you, and vice versa.

As basketball coach and legend John Wooden says, "Show me your friends, and I'll show you your future!" When gearing up for your dream team, clear out the debris (the folks who don't belong) to make room for the treasure that awaits.

My advice for you:

If you want to set your life on fire, seek those who fan the flames, not douse the spark!

My dad says, "Go where you are celebrated, not where you are tolerated."

BUILD YOUR TRIBE

And your tribe builds you.

Within my tribe, I have four types of core teams that help me perform at my peak.

I call them my Fabulous Four.

1. Access Team:

An Access Team ignites your fire, stimulates you to think bigger, and challenges your status quo. These catalysts are 50,000 feet in front of you, teaching you how to cultivate your creativity and catapulting you into the next level of your business and life. I call them the Access Team because they empower you to access your greatness by challenging your thinking and pushing you to rise higher. Your Access Team inspires you to take your next bold move!

When you implement what you learn from these leaders, the sky's the limit on what you can accomplish. Do all you can to gain information from these mentors and gurus: listen to podcasts, read blogs, listen to audiobooks, watch online videos, and so on. If you're the smartest person in the room, you're in the wrong room!

Make a list on the next page of three people you want on your Access Team. Make sure you set up a game plan to bring them into your life and connect with them regularly. Questions you want to ask your Access Team may include: What experience in your life or business forced you to take a next-level risk? What are my blind spots? What advice are you glad you listened to? What advice are you glad you didn't listen to?

BOSS BOLD POWER HABIT

1) My Access Team:
Make a list of three people that you want on your Access Team.

1. _____

2. _____

3. _____

How I will connect with them?

(Example: Podcasts, books, coaching)

_____
_____
_____

BUILD YOUR TRIBE

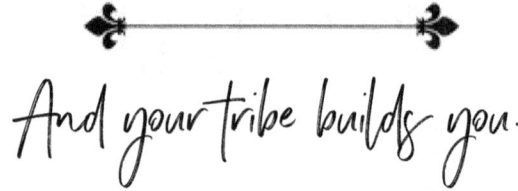

And your tribe builds you.

2) Accountability Team

Ideally, members of your Accountability Team are at about your same career level or a bit in front of you. It works great if it's a two-way street, meaning they keep you accountable to your goals and you do the same for them. With your Accountability Team, you need to ask: Who will keep my feet to the fire and challenge me to be my best every day? Who will hold me accountable to what I say I'm going to do, even when I've lost my motivation?

Power Partner

My business partner and I work closely together and talk daily, but every Tuesday at 9:00 a.m. we check in with each other specifically to make sure our goals are on point. We course-correct along the way and help each other navigate our respective journeys, so that we can focus on the true tasks at hand and power through them.

I love what Proverbs 27:17 says: "Iron sharpens iron, as one person sharpens another."

Feelings will fail you, but a strong Accountability Team will help you power through the difficult days so you get the results you're looking to achieve.

BUILD YOUR TRIBE

And your tribe builds you.

Mastermind Group

Another great resource similar to an Accountability Team is a mastermind group. This is a group that comes together to support one another, help propel each member's business forward, and grow together as leaders. This is an ideal environment to make a bigger impact, drastically increase revenue, and help each other breakthrough limiting beliefs and shift mind-set.

I created a mastermind group with two entrepreneurs whom I respect greatly. We connect monthly via Zoom to run through our goals and review each member's progress from the month before. We bounce ideas off each other, offer support for the objectives of each individual, and encourage each other to keep rocking it out. It has been such a beautiful collaboration. As an entrepreneur it can be a lonely journey unless we intentionally reach out and connect. Masterminds can not only make a big impact on our businesses, but they can also create a phenomenal environment for connection and fulfillment.

BUILD YOUR TRIBE

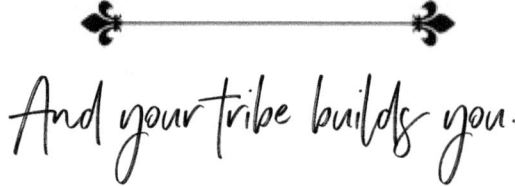

3) Advisor Team

As your empire grows, you'll need to become an expert at leveraging your time. You'll need to outsource aspects of your business if you want to scale, enjoy the journey, and remain big-picture oriented. Your Advisor Team should include any or all of the following: CPA, bookkeeper, personal assistant, financial advisor, business lawyer, insurance broker, personal stylist, social media consultant, business coach, intern, housekeeper, meal prepper, therapist, pastor or spiritual advisor, prayer or meditation partner, nanny, and personal trainer.

Hiring a high-level business coach can be an incredible way to equip you to up-level your A-game! A good coach will be happy to offer you references of other people they've coached. Make sure to ask for them.

Your Advisor Team helps you optimize your week, month, and year so you can work smarter in the areas you're strongest. Yes, you're a crazy-talented Boss. You may feel like you can do it all, and I have no doubt you can, but the real question isn't *can* you do it, but *should* you do it?

You can clean your home; be the full-time chauffeur for your family; cook all the meals; manage your Twitter, Instagram, Facebook, and LinkedIn profiles; update your website; manage your books; make the best financial decisions without help; and run your business. But ask yourself an important question: Would you feel balanced or stressed if you controlled *all* aspects of your life? Your Advisor Team doesn't just help you avoid burnout: they help you save money and time.

Life Hack:

Delegate, delegate, delegate! Stick with your Strength Zone, and leverage your time by becoming a master delegator!

BUILD YOUR TRIBE

And your tribe builds you.

4) Advocate Team

Your Advocate Team consists of the people you're adding value to within your organization or business, including your employees, mentees, team, and interns. This team offers the opportunity to become the ultimate coach and game-changer in someone else's life. Priceless.

These are the people in whom you invest without the expectation of receiving anything in return. I'm a huge believer in the principle of sowing and reaping—meaning, what you sow, you shall reap. But even without considering the reaping aspect, the feeling of pouring into someone selflessly is so fulfilling and life-giving.

I mentioned before that I volunteer at Minnesota Adult and Teen Challenge, which is a faith-based drug and alcohol rehabilitation center. It's been so gratifying investing in the lives of women who are on the road to recovery. It's amazing to see the sparkle in their eyes return as they regain the hope that their circumstances are not the end but the beginning of a whole new chapter. It doesn't get better than witnessing women rewrite their stories to reach their ultimate destiny. To know I've played a small role in that journey brings me to tears when I think about it. When you hear the testimonies of redemption at graduation, you know you're in the right spot!

I also love investing in my Lady Boss Empire tribe and seeing the growth they experience as I coach and empower them with the resources and confidence to shine their true greatness. Case in point: In the early days, one of the leaders of Lady Boss Empire expressed frustration at not having passion or purpose. She wanted to do more and be more, but couldn't quite grasp how to break out of her rut. Together we worked to start her own business and transition from working full time to becoming a stay-at-home mom who offices from home and runs her business passionately. But above and beyond that, she's thankful for the Lady Boss leadership principles.

"Becoming financially free and running my own business trumps it all!" she recently said. "I am not the same girl I was!" It's astounding to watch the growth of women who decide that now is their time and they're done making excuses.

In the end, you can build your tribe however your heart desires, but I like to make sure I'm investing in leaders instead of followers. As a Boss, you've been called to lead a legacy. Your empire is the stuff of legend. When you lead followers, at best, you gain more followers. But when you rise up and lead, collaborate with, and inspire other leaders, the impact you'll have in the world becomes too great to measure. #LeadYourLegacy

BOSS BOLD POWER HABIT

Access Team:	Accountability Team
1. _____	Power Partner _____
2. _____	Mastermind _____
3. _____	Collaborations _____
4. _____	_____
5. _____	

Advisor Team	Advocate Team
1. _____	1. _____
2. _____	2. _____
3. _____	3. _____

Some of my biggest breakthroughs can be traced back to my TRIBE. So, dream BIG, Boss, as you build your Boss Bold Dream Team!

Revisit this chart quarterly to make sure your Dream Team aligns with your biggest and boldest dreams.

Sometimes a Breakup Can Be a Breakthrough

I'd like to get real with you for a moment and share a personal story that, to be honest, still makes me feel a bit vulnerable because of how it affected me at the time. When it happened, it was so unexpected that I felt like I'd been hit by a Mack truck. The reason I want to share this rather uncomfortable story is to equip and prepare you for the kind of surprises that can, and probably will, hit you on the journey to success.

It happened at a time when I had just been happily plugging away at my business, doing my thing, and it seemed like things were all smooth sailing. Suddenly, out of left field, my business partner and close friend informed me via social media that she had jumped ship and decided to go in a completely different direction. She never called, never gave a heads-up, and never bothered to talk through the situation.

I was dumbfounded, blindsided, and, honestly, heartbroken. We had been building together for years, and we were beyond besties; this girl was my soul sister. We were inseparable!

I began questioning myself, wondering what I could have done differently. Was I not enough? Did I not measure up? What's wrong with me? I shut the world out and didn't want to move forward. I felt like my arm was missing.

I started to ask, "Why God?" I took a good amount of time at the lake that summer reading, seeking God, and growing deeper in my faith. One day, while I was out on the lake, I heard a still, small voice inside say, "Nothing happens to you, but for you. This is happening for a reason. Trust me; I've got your back."

Things began to clear in my mind, and I started gaining perspective. On paper, things had been going great, but deep down in my soul I knew I had been playing smaller than what I was capable of because I felt comfortable within my inner circle. Even though we were having a ton of fun, I wasn't being challenged to grow outside my comfort zone. It was an unhealthy dependence that I couldn't see until the connection was stripped in an instant.

In retrospect, I can honestly say I am grateful for what happened. There were countless life lessons that I extracted from the situation. But the main lesson I want to share is that there is purpose in the pain. When life's storms hit, we can choose to get bitter or better; weaker or stronger.

It's always a CHOICE!

> "Not all storms come to disrupt your life;
> some come to clear your path."
> —Stefanie Peters

If this event hadn't happened, I don't believe I would have started my podcast, created my online course, and expanded my reach through speaking. I had no reason to move and expand before, because I was too comfortable. Maybe you are facing a difficult storm in life right now and you're retracting instead of expanding, reacting instead of acting. I want to remind you that there's purpose in the pain, and you are capable of triumphing and coming out even better than before.

Different than I expected, but better than I imagined.

> "If you don't heal what hurt you, you'll bleed on
> people who didn't cut you"
> —Unknown

Real Talk

I always strive to leave people better than I found them. I try my very best to never burn a bridge, even if we agree to disagree. But there will always be people who are jealous or decide to walk away, and even though you do everything in your power to make wrongs right, it will never be good enough.

Later on, that same biz bestie blocked and unfriended me. Sure, it was hurtful, but it wasn't the end of the world. Feel the feelings, cry, but then, as one of my fellow authors, Rachel Hollis, says, "Scrub away the tears and the pain of yesterday and start again. Girl, wash your face!" Be honest about what you need to do to make change. Stop crying about what happened and start taking control of what happens next.

Get up! Rise up! Move on with your life.

"1. Not everyone will take the journey.
2. Not everyone should take the journey.
3. Not everyone can take the journey."
—John C. Maxwell

What I've learned and why it matters:

- Don't force any friendships. Those who are meant to be in your life will show it through their actions.

- Don't let the painful moment turn into a month. Bless and release it and take your power back! Keep your eyes on your own yoga mat. Run YOUR race!

Bless and Release Hack:

Who do you need to forgive to move forward in your life? Is it a friend who deeply hurt you? Do you need to forgive yourself?

Unforgiveness is like drinking poison and expecting the other person to die.

Brain researcher, Dr. Caroline Leaf, has so much insight on the importance of mastering your mindset and the impact that negative thinking, including unforgiveness, can have on the brain.

She writes that 75% to 98% of the illnesses that plague people today are a direct result of their thought life. Fear alone triggers more than 1,400 known physical and chemical responses and activates more than 30 different hormones.

Here's the deal: Your baggage can help heal someone or destroy someone.

Once you are able to process the challenge and move forward whole, you will be able to be a resource for others experiencing a similar situation.

"Every adversity, every failure, every heartache carries with it the seed of an equal or greater benefit."
—Napolean Hill

Be aware: Once you think the issue is behind you, someone may try to pull you back into the drama. If drama comes up, my policy is, "There's the door!" I have no space in my life for the nutty situations people will try to pull you into. If you see drama, you have the freedom to say "delete" in your mind and caringly yet candidly say, "I'm out!" It's a CHOICE!

Reminder: You don't have to rebuild a relationship with everyone you have forgiven. Just because you are at peace doesn't mean they're still not toxic.

I like the way a fellow Lady Boss and podcaster, Jenna Kutcher, says it:

> "Take people's opinions with a grain of salt, add pepper, noodles, some cheese, because mac and cheese matters MORE than what anyone thinks about you. The end."

Amen, sister!

Jenna also puts her "haters" in perspective in a way I love:

"Thank you. Thank you for inspiring me to stick to my conviction. Thank you for proving my point that I shouldn't shy away from the call. Thank you for giving me content to share on my podcast to show the world what keyboard warriors are (and how they can overcome them)."

Here are my two cents: Haters are here to help us, test us, challenge our determination, and push us to up-level! They give us the opportunity to grow in ways not possible without them.

"No one can make you feel inferior without your consent."
—Eleanor Roosevelt

Also, no one can take your peace or joy without your consent. That's an INSIDE job. It's your choice to allow the outside circumstances or people to infiltrate your heart, spirit, and soul.

Feel the feelings because what you bury never dies, but don't get stuck in the muck. Don't allow someone or something to rent space in your head without your consent. Your thought life is critical to the health of your soul.

Reminder: Whatever we focus on EXPANDS! So, focus on your vision!

Set those healthy boundaries (aka defense) and get on with your life.

---

*"People will throw stones at you. Don't throw them back.
Bless them, release them, collect the stones, and build your empire."*
—Stefanie Peters

Okay, I know that was a lot, but we started from the bottom and now we're here. Cue the cheerleaders! Let's get on to how to BUILD your Dream Tribe!

BOSS BOLD POWER MOVE

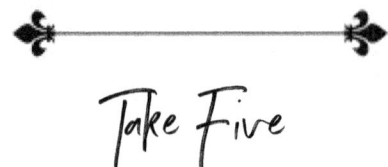

Take Five

List five people in your life that are draining, toxic, or simply have negative energy. Create a strategy to kindly back away and put up healthy boundaries.

1. _____

2. _____

3. _____

4. _____

5. _____

BOSS BOLD POWER MOVE

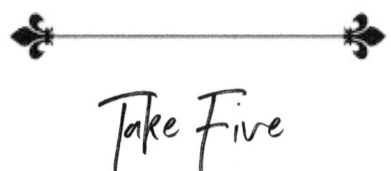

List five people that light you up, encourage you, and emit positive energy. Create a strategy to connect with them.

1. _____

2. _____

3. _____

4. _____

5. _____

AFFIRMATIONS

I am an exceptional leader.

I value connection and trust.

My tribe is successful and abundant.

I have developed an amazing tribe.

My tribe is positive and engaged.

We fully embrace our vision.

We empower each other toward greatness.

"Carve your name on hearts, not tombstones. A legacy is etched into the minds of others and the stories they share about you."
—Shannon L. Alder

PRAYER

Father,

    Thank You for the vision You have given this team. I pray for Your continued guidance and put all we are doing in Your hands. Bless the efforts of each individual and the bonds that are being created. Lord, influence us through your Holy Spirit. I pray for protection and wisdom for this team. I pray for an atmosphere of joy and courage. Mold us, shape us, and grow us to new heights. Teach us to lean on You, O Lord, and each other. Speak Your truth over all that we do. Thank You for Your provision and favor. In Your holy name,

Amen.

RESOURCES

1. *Tribes: We Need You to Lead Us* by Seth Godin
2. *The 17 Indisputable Laws of Teamwork: Embrace Them and Empower Your Team* by John C. Maxwell
3. *Good to Great: Why Some Companies Make the Leap...and Others Don't* by Jim Collins

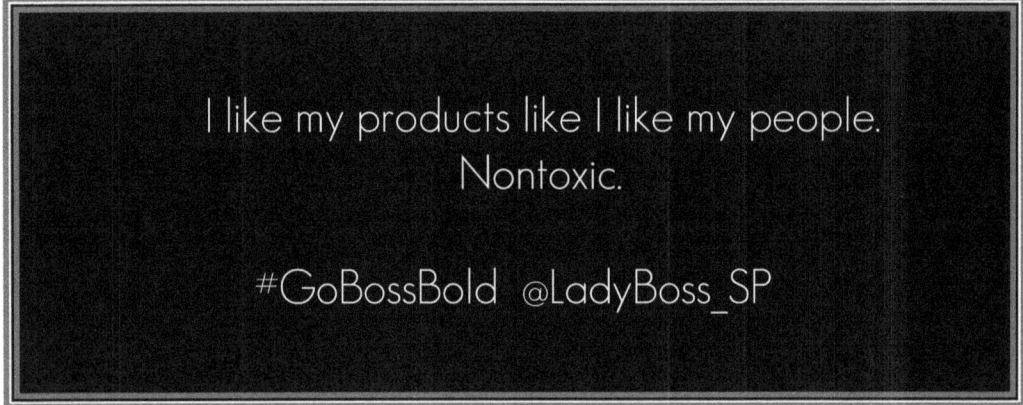

CHAPTER 10

BECOME A LEGEND AND LEAVE YOUR LEGACY

> *"All good men and women must take responsibility to create legacies that will take the next generation to a level we could only imagine."*
> —Jim Rohn

Week 10

BOSS BREAKTHROUGH

"Call 911! We need help and we need help NOW!" screamed my mother.

It was a cold, dreary day in late October 2005, and I was passed out cold. I was 16 a junior in high school, and had been preparing for the most important varsity cross-country meet of my running career. Since I'd been asthmatic all my life and struggled with allergies, I knew in the back of my mind that running on the golf course that particular day could be lethal.

The four-kilometer (2.5 mile) course was extremely wet from recent rain. I found out later that the grounds crew had just sprayed the course with a ton of chemicals. When I arrived at the meet and began my warm-up, I began struggling to breathe. I compensated by using my inhaler, popping a Sudafed, and inhaling several steroids to keep my symptoms at bay. I was determined to run this critical race at optimal performance. But things felt off. When my mother arrived, she insisted I take my nebulizer. I did, and right away my body started to shake.

"Feel the fear and do it anyway," I kept telling myself. So, I stepped up to the starting line after the warm-up and got in the zone as much as I could under the circumstances. I looked down the long starting line and saw the top seven varsity runners from over 20 schools. Some of the best female runners in the state were there.

The starting gun cracked, and off we went. *Focus and forget about the peripherals,* I kept telling myself. *Fight through it! Get after it, girl!* Something felt really wrong, but I kept telling my mind to ignore it.

My dad yelled to encourage me to kick it up at the one-mile marker. He was timing me. I was almost on pace for a personal record. That gave me hope, so I dug deeper and tried to give it everything I had. But then something shifted. I felt like I was kicking it into high gear, but my steps were slowing, and my time was getting farther off. I felt confused and disoriented. But I kept going.

As I passed the two-mile marker, my dad yelled to drive harder. By then, I was significantly off pace. But I couldn't understand why. I thought I was leaving it all on the course! I felt my heart beginning to race, and my breathing was deteriorating. This was a crucial race for me to qualify for state. What was my deal? I was so confused!

BOSS BREAKTHROUGH

I thought the finish line was in sight, finally! *Where have you been all my life?* I thought. I had to run through the shoot, and then I would be finished! The world started to spin. I vaguely remember hearing my dad yell, "Keep going! What are you doing? You've got to finish the race! Get in the shoot!" Wait, what? Hadn't I already crossed the finish line and gone through the shoot? I have absolutely no recollection of what happened in the next five minutes.

My dad told me I never finished the most important cross-country race of my life. He says I staggered eerily over to a post in the finish-line shoot and rested my head on top of it. Dozens of other runners ran by me. Dad yelled again, "You haven't crossed the finish line; you've got twenty yards to go!" More runners passed me. My dad, sensing I was about to pass out, grabbed me and said, "Come on, Sissy. Let's walk it off." My heart was racing way too fast, and my breathing was out of control.

He told me later that as we walked, my lips and body began to turn blue. As he looked at me, my eyes rolled toward the back of my head. I collapsed, and he set me on the ground and screamed for help. Someone finally found my mom.

I hazily remember being carried by four cross-country runners to the medical tent, but no one was there. Someone yelled that the trainer had gone to the clubhouse. There is almost always an ambulance at cross-country races, but not at this one. Meanwhile, time was ticking, and nobody knew how much time I had left.

As they set me down in the clubhouse, my heart seemed to race even faster, and it got harder to breathe. Someone screamed, "Call 911." The trainer yelled for everyone except critical personnel to clear the room. What was happening?

The trainer whispered to my mom and dad, "We've got to get her heart rate down right now or it could stop altogether. *What?! Am I dying?* I thought.

At this point, I felt my heart rate climb to an all-time high I had never experienced. The room began to spin again, and I started to shake. A knife could have cut the heaviness in the room. Not only was my mom crying, but my dad also was crying. They were sure they were watching their daughter die in front of them. The trainer stared at me and my mom with a look of terror.

Suddenly I had this unexplainable peace rush over me. It felt like I was in a fight for my life, yet I also felt like I was seeing the room from above. I was having an out-of-body experience. It was like I was looking down at myself far above the room. There I was, in front of the trainer, gasping for air, gasping for my life!

BOSS BREAKTHROUGH

The serenity I felt is still surreal when I reminisce about that day. I was enveloped by tranquility and complete trust and calm in God. I was at peace.

I started to speak but could still see the situation from above. Then I looked straight at my mom and said, "It's okay. Don't worry. I'm going to be okay." Then I looked at the trainer with absolute clarity and said, "No matter if I stay or if I go, I know Jesus Christ is my personal Lord and Savior. So, no matter what happens, it's all going to be okay." By now my mom was absolutely sobbing, realizing she was losing her baby girl. My dad was in complete shock and disbelief, feeling completely helpless. Where was the ambulance?

But once those words came out of my mouth, I could sense my heart rate beginning to normalize. My breathing began to slow. Color came back into my lips and face.

I'll spare you the details of the recovery process, but what I will say is that my body wasn't used to the amount of drugs being pumped into me, so it started to react violently. But once my body got to the point of stabilization, I sat in complete shock at what had happened. Once I got my bearings, I slowly limped to the car. I felt like a weak, elderly woman, exhausted from that horrendous experience.

THE PARADIGM SHIFT FROM SUCCESS TO SIGNIFICANCE

I sank into the seat of my car, still wracked with pain from the convulsions. Yet my thoughts were crystal clear. I suddenly saw my life from a new perspective with complete clarity. I told my parents, "I've been totally chasing the wrong goals. The cross-country titles I've relentlessly pursued, the four-point grade point average, the varsity letter jacket, National Honor Society, now seem so hollow. Mom and Dad, what truly matters is my relationship with God and how I make an impact in people's lives. I really can't take much else with me when I die."

As I think back on the day I almost lost my life, I am in awe and astounded at how God turned a near-death experience into a complete paradigm shift—one that I needed if I was going to fulfill the purpose He placed in my heart. As horrid as the experience was, I'm so grateful and humbled that He allowed me to stay here and to gain the insight I did. Honestly, that is exactly what this stubborn girl needed to shake her up and show her the light.

BOSS BOLD
POWER PRINCIPLE

Many of us wonder about the spiritual purpose for our lives. Why are we here? What is our purpose? My near-death experience gave me the perspective to ask God the big questions in life and to realize how fleeting it all is. Without having gone through it, I might never have realized the true strength of my spirit and the fragility of my body, of the *human* body—we are so temporary but so powerful when we harness our God-given gifts and purpose.

Have *you* truly examined your talents, passions, and who you were created to be? I've found that no matter where we are in life, the resources, connections, and strength to do what we're called to do will be provided to us.

> *Once you've tasted significance, success will never completely satisfy you. What type of legacy are you leaving? If our dreams only impact us, then we need to check our priorities. What is our grander purpose? How do we want to be remembered?*

When we do our part with the gifts we're given, doors will open that no man, woman, or situation can shut! And when we continue to use what we're given, we are given infinitely more in return. Call me crazy, but I believe we are spiritual beings having a human experience. (Stick with me here—I promise I'm not jumping off the deep end. To live your ultimate purpose you need to hear this.) I personally believe that our ultimate power source is God. If we unplug and don't connect with our spiritual selves, we quickly lose heart, become complacent, and lose our way. Life becomes tasteless, and our fire dies.

Until I made God the CEO of my business and life, I was working hard but lacked the focus and purpose only He can bring. Before God was the center of my business, I felt like the driver with no idea where I was going. When someone pointed out that I was going in the wrong direction, I replied, "But I'm making great time!" People, businesses, and life will sometimes fail us, but God never will.

BOSS BOLD POWER PRINCIPLE

This point was made even clearer to me recently. I was reading a book called *Fervent*, by Priscilla Shirer, and this passage in Key #6 was life-changing. It reads:

> *"If I were your enemy, I'd magnify your fears, making them appear insurmountable, intimidating you with enough worries until avoiding them becomes your driving motivation. I would use anxiety to cripple you, to paralyze you, leaving you indecisive, clinging to safety and sameness, always on the defensive because of what might happen. When you hear the word faith, all I'd want you to hear is 'unnecessary risk.'"*

I've coached hundreds of Bosses through the years. I believe the number one reason people slam on their brakes and stop pursuing their passion is because of this loathsome thing called fear. We fear the unknown, we fear what people will think, and we fear that we don't have what it takes.

Perhaps your fearful thoughts sound something like this: What if I can't do it? What if pursuing my destiny is a total waste of my time and energy? I'm not ready. I don't think I have what it takes to make my dream a reality. Better to be safe than sorry.

But, here's the deal: We have two options:

1) We can become paralyzed by fear and stop moving forward, or
2) We can step out in faith, feel the fear, and get after it, regardless of our feelings.

BOSS BOLD
POWER PRINCIPLE

Playing it safe never writes the history books!

It's time to get fed up with our fear and get over it. Our minds play stupid, lethal tricks on us, and fear is a frontline weapon that cripples us Bosses. But that is precisely what faith is. When our fears tell us we can't, faith is designed to remind us that we can and we must!

Pastor John Bevere said, "You will not be held accountable for what you did here on earth, but for what you were called to do on earth!"

If that isn't a paradigm shift I don't know what is. Sometimes I can get so wrapped up in not moving fast enough or thinking someone else's path looks sexier or more enticing than mine, but at the end of the day nothing can replace the feeling that you gave it your all running *your* race.

We are performing for an audience of One.

BOSS BOLD POWER PRINCIPLE

Terri Savelle Foy, an inspirational speaker, was given an assignment in high school that shifted her perspective forever:

"Class, I want you to get out a sheet of paper and write your full name at the top," said Terri's high school English teacher, Mrs. Sawyer. "Underneath your name, write your birth date, and last night's date. Now, I want each of you to write your own obituary. What would people say about you at your funeral?" Mrs. Sawyer bluntly asked.

"Give it some thought," she said. "What would your parents say about you? How would your siblings describe you? How would your closest friends describe your personality? How did you spend your time? What were you known for? Who did you help? What would your pastor say about you?"

She continued, "Class, before you start, I don't want you to write what you've done up to this time in your life. I don't want you to write how your friends and family would currently describe you. I want you to write what you want said about you at your funeral someday."

Mrs. Sawyer held out her hand to collect the obituaries and made this statement, "Students, you have not only written your obituaries, you've written your dreams.... Now, go live them."

Terri said this assignment was more than thought-provoking; it was life-changing, destiny-pointing, and discipline-provoking.

Wow! What a profound and life-altering assignment. But it's not for high school students alone; it's for you. It's for anyone and everyone who wants to live a life designed to succeed on purpose. It's for anyone who longs to make the years matter and the days count. It's for you today to trigger self-motivation like never before.

When you come to the end of your life and you look back, what do you want people to say about you? How would they describe you? What would they say you did during your time on earth? Did you make a difference in anyone's life? Were you focused on making an impact? Did you do all the things you said you would do? Did you live a full life? Did you have a vision before you? Did you fully enjoy the value of each day?

BOSS BOLD POWER MOVE

Let's do Mrs. Sawyer's assignment!

Obituary

Write what you want to be said about you: who you were, how you made an impact, and the legacy you have left on this world.

Name _____

DOB: _____

Last Night's Date: _____

_____
_____
_____
_____
_____
_____
_____
_____
_____
_____
_____
_____

I will echo what Mrs. Sawyer said,
"You have not only written your obituaries,
you've written your dreams.... Now, go live them."

BOSS BOLD POWER MOVE

Now I want you to take it a step further.... In order to have complete clarity on the legacy you want to leave, it's imperative to nail out your Boss Bold mission statement!

"Without a mission statement, you may get to the top of the ladder and then realize it was leaning against the wrong building."

—Dave Ramsey

"Creating and integrating an empowering personal mission statement is one of the most important investments we can make."

—Stephen Covey

"The most extraordinary people in the world today don't have a career. They have a mission."

—Vishen Lakhiani

Six Simple Steps to Create Your Boss Bold Mission Statement

(Write down everything that comes to mind on the next page and fill out the chart.)

Boss Bold Steps	Boss Bold Insights	Boss Bold Clarity

1) Ask questions	Dig in DEEP:
	    Who are you?
	    What is your purpose? Why?
	    How do you want to make an impact?
	    Whom do you want to empower?
	    How do you want to equip them?
		Your unique gift:
		• How are you different?
		• What's your secret sauce?
		• What is your zone of genius?
		• How can you serve in a way unique to your gifts?

2) Brainstorm based on your answers	What answers sparked your soul? What answers ignited your passion for life?	Now get GOING ----- on the next page ...
3) Pick YOUR power words/ phrases	Brain dump here: • How do you want to brand it? Name recognition, slogan, motto	Now narrow it down:
4) Build your Boss Bold mission statement	Best Motto/Phrases:	Craft your unique statement:
5) Get insight from mentor/coach	Share for feedback and how you can improve it	Ask your inner circle how this ignites their life/purpose?
6) Design and finalize	Implement insights and shift according to what resonates with you	Create your final mission statement, Boss Up and lead with intention

Your Mission Statement

Go back to the questions in the previous chart and fill out your answers below.

Boss Bold Steps	Boss Bold Insights	Boss Bold Clarity
1)		
2)		
3)		
4)		
5)		
6)		

Examples of Mission Statements:

1. *"To be a teacher. And to be known for inspiring my students to be more than they thought they could be."*
   —Oprah Winfrey
2. *"Every day I equip leaders to unapologetically live out their divine destiny & glorify God."*
   —Stefanie Peters
3. *"To make people happy."*
   —Walt Disney
4. *"Not merely to survive, but to thrive; and to do so with some passion, some compassion, some humor, and some style."*
   —Maya Angelou
5. *"To use my gifts of intelligence, charisma, and serial optimism to cultivate the self-worth and net-worth of women around the world."*
   —Amanda Steinberg, Dailyworth.com

My Mission Statement

_____
_____
_____
_____
_____
_____
_____
_____

*P.S. - There is no right or wrong when it comes to writing your personal mission statement because it is PERSONAL. You can create a three word or three-sentence statement. It's your call, boss!! But my two cents: Less is more!

Add your mission statement to your Thank You Card and your vision board and read it out loud daily. Revisit your mission statement quarterly and ask God to reveal how you can live out your mission in a bigger, bolder way every day.

Ephesians 3:20-21 (NIV)
"Now to Him who is able to do immeasurably more than all we ask or imagine, according to His power that is at work within us, to Him be glory in the church and in Christ Jesus throughout all generations, forever and ever! Amen."

Today is the only day you have to start the life you've always dreamed. You don't have to do everything on your list, but you have to start somewhere. Do something. Stop procrastinating. Choose purpose over perfection, rise up, and beat the game of fear. We are born for such a time as this.

There you have it, Boss. It's time to take massive action toward your destiny—and right now. It's time to leave your mark. A Boss's vision is much bigger than one that can be accomplished by a single person. When we all dare to come together to do the "impossible," we become legends. We crush the status quo and illuminate the legacy of possibility for generations. If you've been praying for a sign, this is it. Step up and lead the Boss Life Revolution.

"That is your legacy on this Earth when you leave this Earth: how many hearts you touched."
—Patti Davis

AFFIRMATIONS

I AM a person of influence. I influence others to strive towards their own dreams, to reach beyond previous limitations, and to be bold in their God-sized mission.

I am disciplined, focused, and present to everything that God wants me to receive.

I am valuable, I am courageous and wise. I am fulfilled.

My words are anointed.

My soul is blessed.

My prayers and praise are dangerous.

My destiny is unstoppable.

PRAYER

Jesus,

    Thank You for the space that You have me in right now, a space that has caused me to stretch and grow and dig deep. I pray that You continue to elevate my mind, renew my spirit, and position my heart towards You and my purpose on this earth. Link arms with me, O Lord, and teach me to live, love, and lead like You. Amen.

RESOURCES

1. *Your Legacy: The Greatest Gift* by Dr. James Dobson
2. *The Compound Effect* by Darren Hardy
3. *The Legacy Journey: A Radical View of Biblical Wealth and Generosity* by Dave Ramsey

> *"Bosses that leave a legacy don't see the seed; they see the tree, and then they envision the forest."*
> —Stefanie Peters
>
> #GoBossBold @LadyBoss_SP

MY TOP 100 LIVE LIFE LIST

LIVE LIST OATH:

I solemnly swear to build memories that last a lifetime.

I vow to make an impression on the world, not the couch.

I promise to dream God-sized goals.

And make them my reality!

_____ _____
Sign   Date

HERE IS YOUR PLACE TO DREAM BIG, BOSS

This is your opportunity to put pen to paper and write your LIVE list; the things you want to accomplish while you are here on this planet!

Places I will go		
Places I will go	Target date to achieve	Completed
1.		
2.		
3.		
4.		
5.		
6.		
7.		
8.		
9.		
10.		

11.		
12.		
13.		
14.		
15.		
16.		
17.		
18.		
19.		
20.		
21.		
22.		
23.		
24.		
25.		

The one place I will for sure go this year:_____

Things I will do

Things I will do	Target date to achieve	Completed
1.		
2.		
3.		
4.		
5.		
6.		
7.		
8.		
9.		
10.		
11.		
12.		
13.		
14.		
15.		

16.		
17.		
18.		
19.		
20.		
21.		
22.		
23.		
24.		
25.		

The thing that I will do this year: _____

This matters to me because: _____

Things I will have

Things I will have	Target date to achieve	Completed
1.		
2.		
3.		
4.		
5.		
6.		
7.		
8.		
9.		
10.		
11.		
12.		
13.		
14.		
15.		

16.		
17.		
18.		
19.		
20.		
21.		
22.		
23.		
24.		
25.		

The thing that I will have this year:_____

I want this because:_____

Adventures I will experience

Adventures	Target date to achieve	Completed
1.		
2.		
3.		
4.		
5.		
6.		
7.		
8.		
9.		
10.		
11.		
12.		
13.		
14.		
15.		

16.		
17.		
18.		
19.		
20.		
21.		
22.		
23.		
24.		
25.		

The adventure I will experience this year is:_____

This adventure is important because:_____

LIVE LIST IDEAS

Places I will go!

On a Mediterranean cruise

The Dead Sea

Snorkeling

To a nude beach

White water rafting

On a gondola in Venice, Italy

The Coliseum in Rome

The Grand Canyon and walk the Sky Walk

The Tower of London

The Summer Olympics

A Broadway show in New York

Disney with my kids

Bora Bora

Paris

The northern woods for a hike by the waterfalls

LIVE LIST IDEAS

Things I will do!

Write a book

Run a marathon

Kiss in the rain

Learn another language

Start a business

Launch a blog

Buy an investment property

Meet the president

Start a foundation

Go on a mission trip

Visit all U.S. states

Appear on the cover of a magazine

Complete a triathlon

Volunteer abroad

Host a charity event

Get married to my soulmate

Burn my mortgage

LIVE LIST IDEAS

Things I will have/give!

Vacation home
Donate a car to my favorite foundation
An incredible relationship with my spouse
A condo in the Florida keys
A vacation home in the mountains
A beach house and turn it into an Airbnb
Becoming an expert in ...
The memory of going skinny dipping
A debt-free life
A pet adopted from the Humane Society
Give one-year tuition to a college student
Tip someone $1,000
Give my parents the gift of a vacation in Tahiti for their 50th wedding anniversary
Give away a get-away to my besties at my vacation home

LIVE LIST IDEAS

Adventures I will experience!

Take an African safari

See the northern lights

Walk along the Great Wall of China

Snorkel at the Great Barrier Reef

Ride a Venetian gondola

View Paris from atop the Eiffel Tower

Climb a tall mountain

Backpack through Europe

Fly a hot air balloon

Sleep underneath the stars

Swim with the dolphins

Sit courtside at a basketball game

Fly an airplane

Skydive

Study abroad

Boss Life Blueprint

"If you don't design your own life plan, chances are you will fall into someone else's plan. And guess what they have planned for you? Not much!"

—Jim Rohn

My Word for the year: _____

My Scripture / Mantra for the year: _____

Personal Development Plan

Quarter 1:	Quarter 2:

Top Three Goals:
   1. _____
   2. _____
   3. _____
 	
Books I will read:
 	
Event I will attend:
 	
Courses/classes I will take:
	Top Three Goals:
	   1. _____
	   2. _____
	   3. _____
	
	Books I will read:
	
	Event I will attend:
	
	Courses/classes I will take:

Quarter 3:	Quarter 4:

Top three goals:
   1. _____
   2. _____
   3. _____
 	
Books I will read:
 	
Event I will attend:
 	
Courses/classes I will take:
	Top three goals:
	   1. _____
	   2. _____
	   3. _____
	
	Books I will read:
	
	Event I will attend:
	
	Courses/classes I will take:

My Mission Statement: _____

My top ten goals for the year: My goal date:

1. _____   _____
2. _____   _____
3. _____   _____
4. _____   _____
5. _____   _____
6. _____   _____
7. _____   _____
8. _____   _____
9. _____   _____
10. _____   _____

My Dream Team

You need to hang out with people who fit your future, not your history!

Access Team: Accountability Team:

1. _____   1. Power Partner: _____
2. _____   2. Mastermind: _____
3. _____   3. Collaborations: _____

Advisor Team: Advocate Team:

1. _____   1. _____
2. _____   2. _____
3. _____   3. _____
4. _____
5. _____

OUT OF MY LEAGUE LUNCHES
Meet with one person who is out of your league once a month.

1. _____
2. _____
3. _____
4. _____
5. _____
6. _____

7. _____
8. _____
9. _____
10. _____
11. _____
12. _____

My Weekly Power Plan

If getting up 30 minutes earlier to pursue your God-sized dream seems overwhelming, you've either got the wrong dream or you're just pretending you have one. #BossUP

My daily Dream Routine:

1. _____
2. _____
3. _____

Three things I will stop doing to create space for my goals:

1. _____
2. _____
3. _____

Top three goals
1. _____
2. _____
3. _____

Number of Power Hours I will time block for:

_____
_____
_____

Schedule your Power Hours below:

#CreateSpace	What's your reward for accomplishing this? #CelebrateTheSmallWins
Monday:	
Tuesday:	
Wednesday:	
Thursday:	
Friday:	
Saturday:	
Sunday:	

"You will never change your life until you change something you do daily; the secret of your success is found in your daily routine."
—John C Maxwell

My Definition of a Boss:

My One-Year Vision:

My Five-Year Vision:

My Ten-Year Vision:

My five "I am" statements:
1. _____
2. _____
3. _____
4. _____
5. _____

My five gratitudes
1. _____
2. _____
3. _____
4. _____
5. _____

If I FIRED my FEAR I would:

Within 24 hours I will:

My Power Partner who will keep me accountable:

Boss Bold Quarterly Check-In

*Top three WINS of the quarter:
 1. _____
 2. _____
 3. _____

*Top three course corrections I need to implement to move the needle in the coming quarter:
 1. _____
 2. _____
 3. _____

*Top three goals I will accomplish this year to make it my BEST year yet:
 1. _____
 2. _____
 3. _____

What doors do I need to close this quarter that are no longer serving me? What is draining me of energy? What do I need to bless and release?

How can I step into my power this quarter & live UNAPOLOGETICALLY?

BOSS BOLD BLISSFUL LIFE

If it's not an income-producing or a joy producing activity: Delegate, automate, or eliminate it!
Eradicate your joy stealers!

What drains me of my energy?
1. _____
2. _____
3. _____
4. _____

How will I ditch, delete, or reframe these?
1. _____
2. _____
3. _____
4. _____

What steals my joy?
1. _____
2. _____
3. _____
4. _____

How will I course correct these joy stealers?
1. _____
2. _____
3. _____
4. _____

What are my best ROI activities?
1. _____
2. _____
3. _____
4. _____

How can I implement these into my daily life?
1. _____
2. _____
3. _____
4. _____

What brings me joy?
1. _____
2. _____
3. _____
4. _____

How can I add these into my life more often?
1. _____
2. _____
3. _____
4. _____

CITATIONS

1. "Tyler Perry Biography." *Encyclopedia of World Biography*, Advameg, Inc., www.notablebiographies.com/newsmakers2/2006-Le-Ra/Perry-Tyler.html.

2. Arnold, Michael, et al. "Tyler Perry Biography - Inspired by Oprah, Perseverance Paid Off, Concentrated on Madea Character." *Review, York, Scholastic, and Press - JRank Articles*, biography.jrank.org/pages/2872/Perry-Tyler.html.

3. Whelan, Fred, and Gladys Stone. "Lou Holtz's Compelling Quest to Do 107 Things Before He Died." *HuffPost*, HuffPost, 9 Dec. 2010, www.huffpost.com/entry/lou-holtzs-compelling-que_b_794675.

4. Reports, Staff. "Collected Wisdom: Former Notre Dame Coach Lou Holtz Sets High Standards." *NewsOK.com*, NewsOK, 2 Apr. 2017, newsok.com/article/5543922/collected-wisdom-former-notre-dame-coach-lou-holtz-sets-high-standards.

5. "Tim Tebow Dismisses Media: 'I Don't Care What They Write About Me'." *CNS News*, 27 Feb. 2017, www.cnsnews.com/blog/michael-morris/tebow-addresses-critical-media-baseball-pursuit-i-dont-care-what-they-write

6. "Tim Tebow Could Set Precedent If He Never Starts Another NFL Game." *The Idea Log*, blogs.denverpost.com/broncos/2013/05/02/tim-tebow-could-set-precedence-if-he-never-starts-another-nfl-game/19265/.

7. Jenny Dearborn, jennydearborn.com/give-your-brain-a-break/.

About the Author

Stefanie Peters is a national speaker, author, and serial entrepreneur. She started her first business at the age of eighteen. She shattered the glass ceiling and became the youngest female executive in one of the fastest-growing companies in North America. Stefanie was determined to help women find financial freedom and independence. As her movement grew, she founded Lady Boss Empire, an empowerment platform and resource center for female entrepreneurs. She is the host of *The Boss Life Podcast*, creator of the online course The Boss Life Blueprint, certified John C Maxwell coach, and a savvy real estate investor.

Looking for ongoing INSPIRATION, insight, and powerful tools to take your business and life to the next level?

Tune into The Boss Life Podcast and make sure to take advantage of The Boss Life Blueprint online course!
Check it out at www.TheBossLife.tv

SCHEDULE STEFANIE TO SPEAK AT YOUR NEXT EVENT!

Stefanie Peters is guaranteed to deliver an inspiring, entertaining, and life-changing message! She is a certified speaker, coached by her mentor, best-selling author John C. Maxwell. For more than a decade, Stefanie has been inspiring and teaching audiences to:

- Unlock their **inner greatness**
- **Break through** barriers and self-doubt
- Take strategic **actions** to get **results**

Through her specific strategies, power plan, and hilarious real-life stories, Stefanie ignites audiences to take their lives and businesses to the next level!

FOR MORE INFORMATION

Visit www.thebosslife.tv
or contact Stefanie directly at
Stefanie@thebosslife.tv.

www.ingramcontent.com/pod-product-compliance
Lightning Source LLC
Chambersburg PA
CBHW081159230426
43666CB00016B/2864